25 Great Bike Rides of the Twin Cities

by
Jonathan Poppele

Adventure Publications, Inc.
Cambridge, MN

Dedication

To my mom—my loyal tandem stoker and my cycling companion for over 35 years.

Acknowledgements

I would first and foremost like to thank my family. Thanks to my parents, Meredith and Richard, for introducing me to cycling at a young age and leading me on rides all across the Twin Cities while I was growing up. Thanks to my sister, Jessica, and my brother, Eric, for inspiring me through their own cycling adventures and fueling my love for this beautiful sport. A very special thank you also to Dan Casebeer and all of my teammates at the Saint Paul Bicycle Racing Club for their years of encouragement, mentoring and camaraderie. My years of riding and racing with you transformed my view of what was possible for me and for others. Thanks to the members of the Twin Cities Bicycling Club for their dedication to sharing the sport of cycling, and to all those who joined me as I road-tested routes for this book. Finally, a special thanks to the team at Adventure Publications for envisioning this book and working with me to make it a reality.

Edited by Brett Ortler
Cover and book design by Lora Westberg

Trail maps by Peter May
Front Cover: all photos by Jonathan Poppele except for bottom right photo by Blake Hoena

All other photos by Jonathan Poppele and Adventure Publications staff

Copyright 2013 by Jonathan Poppele
Published by Adventure Publications, Inc.
820 Cleveland Street South
Cambridge, MN 55008
800-678-7006
www.adventurepublications.net
All rights reserved
Printed in China
ISBN: 978-1-59193-298-7

Table of Contents:

Introduction

Routes

Central Metro

Northern Metro

Eastern Metro

Southern Metro

Western Metro

About the Author

A Biking Destination

The Twin Cities is one of the best places in the country to bike. Despite our long winters, we have a cycling-friendly culture and what is arguably the most extensive network of off-street bike trails in America. According to the Census Bureau, we have the second-highest percentage of bike commuters in the U.S., second only to Portland, Oregon. And, in 2011, *Bicycling* magazine named Minneapolis the most bike-friendly city in America, ranking us ahead of such cycling meccas as Portland, Oregon; Boulder, Colorado; and Seattle, Washington.

I began cycling on the bike trails in and around the Twin Cities as a child in the 1970s. Following along behind my parents and siblings on my orange banana-seat single speed, I got my first taste of what would become a life-long love. As a teenager, I rode thousands of miles each year, exploring every corner of the metro area. Over the course of three decades, I have watched our region's exceptional network of bike trails take shape.

Even though the Twin Cities metro area is home to dozens of regional and state trails and hundreds of miles of local bike paths, it can still be difficult to link together interesting, fun rides. In this book, I have created 25 family-friendly bike rides that draw on my 35 years of cycling experience and the tens of thousands of miles I've biked in the Twin Cities metro area.

Most of the rides in this book are between 10 and 20 miles in length and predominantly follow off-street bike paths. More than three-quarters of the routes are loops, with a handful of out-and-back, lollipop- and dumbbell-shaped routes mixed in for variety. In addition, most routes include suggestions for shortening or lengthening the ride, and many connect with other routes in the book.

If you are new to bicycling in the Twin Cities, this book will provide you with many great routes to explore. Even if you are a seasoned cyclist, this book will introduce you to new trails, new routes, and new ways to get the most out of your cycling adventures.

Cycling Is for Everyone

Cycling is truly a lifelong sport. I started going on bike rides together with my family when I was six years old. My one-speed coaster-brake bike never seemed like a limitation as I accompanied my family along the bike trails of the Minneapolis Grand Rounds to Lake Nokomis for a picnic and a swim. Today as I ride around the lakes, I see children even younger than I was enjoying time with their parents. I also see infants in bike trailers, preschoolers on "trail-a-bikes," and youngsters on the backs of tandems.

When I began riding as a child, my parents were about the age I am now. We have never stopped riding together as a family. In 1996, my brother, my parents, my sister and I all celebrated my dad's 60th birthday by riding 100 miles in the Minnesota Ironman Bike Ride. My mom and I rode an inexpensive tandem bicycle that we got for the occasion. Sixteen years later, we still have the tandem. Today, my mother deals with Parkinson's and cannot comfortably balance on a solo bicycle—but we still ride our tandem.

Cycling can also be a very inexpensive sport. It is true that bicycling is inherently equipment-intensive, and it is possible to spend a great deal of money on gear. At one point in my early-twenties, I purchased two different bicycles that each cost more than any car I have ever owned. That may say more about the cars I drive than the bikes I ride, but it still highlights how pricey equipment can be. Add to that specialty clothing, clip-in shoes and pedals, bike computers and other accessories, and the costs can be truly exorbitant.

But good, basic equipment need not cost a great deal of money, and it can last a long, long time. Good, used bicycles are easy to find, and a high-quality new bicycle can be an investment that lasts many decades. I still have those two bikes I bought nearly 20 years ago, and I still use them as my primary means of transportation most of the year. Meanwhile, I have replaced my car four times. Other than a bike helmet, most of the accessories are genuinely optional. Some may enhance efficiency or comfort, but you don't need them in order to enjoy riding your bike.

A Note about Safety

Cycling carries with it some inherent risks. Most of us experienced at least a few skinned knees when we first learned to ride a bike, and some of us have experienced more serious spills. I have fallen off my bike many times and the vast majority of those "accidents" were the result of me doing something foolish. Careful riding and a few basic precautions can prevent most accidents and keep your rides safe and fun.

Wear a Helmet

The single most important safety rule is to wear a helmet. I consider this absolutely essential. Please excuse me for harping on this point a bit. While most accidents are avoidable, there is simply no reason to take chances with your one and only brain. I have walked away from several crashes that would have sent me to the hospital had I not been wearing my helmet. Sadly, I have had friends who were seriously injured when they were not wearing helmets. A bike-shop co-worker of mine had his jaw wired shut for six weeks after a stick he rode over flipped up and jammed in his front wheel, sending him over the handlebars. A childhood acquaintance suffered a brain injury after being struck by a speeding car on the residential street in front of his house, leaving him with a serious learning disability.

No matter where you ride, how fast you ride, or how good of a rider you are, accidents happen. A bicycle helmet is the best "health insurance" policy you can have. I won't so much as ride down to the end of the block without wearing a helmet. There's just no reason to take the risk. Please always wear a helmet and make sure your kids always wear theirs. And when you do, make sure that your helmet is the proper size and that it is correctly fitted.

Maintain Your Bike

Before heading out on a ride, make sure your bike is in good working order. Of greatest importance, make sure that the wheels are properly secured and the brakes are working correctly. It is a good idea to have your bike tuned up by a skilled mechanic at least once each year. If you prefer to take care of your own equipment, there are some excellent books and classes available on bike maintenance.

Know Your Brakes

Before you go, make sure you are comfortable with your bike's brakes. Learning how to safely slow down and stop is the most important riding technique. Young riders especially should practice slowing and stopping under controlled conditions before venturing out onto unknown trails. Be extra cautious on steep hills. Slowing and stopping from high speeds requires a different technique. Build up your skill and confidence gradually. Finally, if you get on a different bike, try out the brakes before heading off on a ride. An experienced member of one of the local cycling clubs recently sent himself over the handlebars on a borrowed bike because the brakes behaved differently than what he was used to.

Watch out for Wood, Metal and Painted Surfaces while Riding

Wood, metal and painted surfaces can become very slippery when wet—and sometimes even when they are dry. Use extra caution when crossing wooden bridges, manhole covers and painted crosswalks. It is best to ride in a straight line across these surfaces. Also, use extra caution when crossing railroad tracks. Crossing tracks at an angle can cause a wheel to jam, leading to a fall. Whenever possible, cross tracks at a right angle.

Trail Safety Tips

Most of the rides in this book are along bike trails. Bike trails offer many advantages over street riding, especially for families. The trails are segregated from traffic, have smoother surfaces and often have fewer intersections. However, trails are not without risks. Here are a few guidelines for safe riding on bike trails:

- Keep it slow: Most bike trails are designed for a traffic speed of less than 15 mph. Some trails, like those that circle the lakes of Minneapolis, have a posted speed limit of 10 mph. This makes trails ideal for families out to enjoy a casual ride.

- Yield to other trail users: Trail regulations vary, but most cities and counties require bicycles to yield to all other trail users. Even where this isn't the law, it is good courtesy. Always give walkers, joggers, in-line skaters, and horses (yes, there are some trails that allow horses) the right of way.

- Alert other trail users: When approaching other trail users, always announce your presence. The customary alert when overtaking another trail user on their left side is to call out "On your left." When approaching another trail user from the front who has not noticed you, it is polite to call out a quick "Hello" or "Pardon me." A bicycle bell is another friendly way of alerting other trail users to your presence.

- Yield to cars: The most dangerous places along bike trails are where they cross roads and streets. At some street crossings, cyclists technically have the right-of-way, but not all drivers know this and being in the right won't protect you in a collision. Where trails run parallel to roads, drivers on cross streets often pull past the trail when approaching intersections, cutting off bike traffic. When approaching any street intersection, always assume that there are cars coming, and always assume that they are not going to stop.

- Beware of hazards and announce them: Keep an eye out for hazards along the trail, including overhanging branches, debris, gates and awkward curb cuts. Announce any hazards you see to those riding behind you, as their view of the trail may be blocked by you.
- Stop safely: If you are riding with others, always announce when you are slowing or stopping. If you stop along a trail, get completely off the trail so you do not block traffic.

What Else to Bring with You

In addition to a helmet, there are a few other things you may want to have with you on a ride.

- A water bottle and a snack: Most of these rides have drinking fountains at the ride start and some have food available along the route, but you may wish to bring your own. If you drink a great deal of water while working out, make sure to replenish your electrolytes, not just water. Hyponatremia—low blood sodium—is much more common among recreational endurance athletes than dehydration, and it is much more dangerous. If you drink more than one large bottle of water on a ride, include a sports drink that has electrolytes.
- Bike computer: A bicycle computer will tell you how far you have traveled, which can be very helpful for following cue sheets. Computers range in price from quite inexpensive to exorbitant. Properly calibrated, even the least expensive device can give you an accurate measure of speed and distance. There are also several smartphone apps that can serve as a bike computer.
- Bike shorts: Of all the pieces of specialized cycling clothing, the only one that I wear on all of my rides is a pair of bike shorts. Padded, spandex bike shorts are designed to minimize chafing and pressure points from seams on your seat. If you ride occasionally, you may find them a pleasant addition to your wardrobe. If you ride frequently, you may soon wonder how you ever got by without them.
- Spare tube, pump, and patch kit: Flat tires are the most common mechanical breakdown on a bike ride. Having a spare along—and knowing how to change a flat—can make the difference between a ten-minute delay and a ten-mile walk. Even if you don't know how to change a flat, carry a spare tube for your bike—there is a good chance that another trail user will be able to help you.

- Sunscreen: Even on cloudy days, cyclists get a lot of UV exposure. Guidelines for cyclists recommend using a broad-spectrum sunscreen with an SPF of at least 15 on all exposed skin, including the lips. Reapply sunscreen frequently.
- Cell phone: A phone can be handy in an emergency or to coordinate with family members, but it is never safe to talk on a phone while riding. If you bring a phone along, consider keeping it turned off until you need it.

How to Use this Book

The 25 rides in this book are organized by their location in the Twin Cities area. In all, there are five sections: Central, Northern, Eastern, Southern and Western. Because some rides begin in one part of the metro and end in another, I used a ride's starting point to determine its region. The **overview map** on page 13 gives a rough idea of where the rides are in the Twin Cities.

Each account begins with the essential information for that ride: the cities the route passes through, the ride length (including the length of alternate options), tips for that specific ride, and considerations to keep in mind along the way. Navigation is made as easy as possible thanks to a detailed map and step-by-step directions for the entire ride. When a route includes a turn that is easy to overlook, I have made a note in the text to **Watch for this turn**. In addition, points of interest along the route are noted and we've also included a list of extended activities in the area.

Trail Environment For a quick glance at what you can expect for the general surroundings of each trail, look for the Trail Environment section. This map will tell you if that trail is mostly through parks, through residential areas, or along busy streets. You may then elect to ride the trail that fits your mood for the day, or you may choose to do only parts of the trail, perhaps the park portion, for example. It also includes GPS coordinates for the ride start, the rest stops and points of interest along the way.

Jon's Top Picks

If you are trying to figure out which routes to start with, here are some of my suggestions. I listed routes that I think are the most family friendly, rides that have some fun extended activities, and ones for more experienced bikers. Plus, I included of list of rides that will take you to some of those icons of the Twin Cities as well as routes for the nature lovers.

Family Friendly Rides

These are the best routes for children on single-speed bikes or riders towing trailers. They are nearly flat and follow wide, smooth trails. These are also great for rollerblading.

1. Concord by the Mississippi (page 128)
2. Gateway Trail (page 80)
3. Cedar Lake Express (page 140)
4. Midtown Lollipop (page 26)
5. Rush Creek Lollipop (page 56)

Easy Rides to Turn into a Day Trip

These routes can easily be turned into full day trips. They include one or more great opportunities for family outings at the start or along the way.

1. Around the Zoo (page 110)
2. Trails to Light Rails (page 38)
3. Elm Creek Park (page 146)
4. Lake Elmo Dumbbell (page 92)
5. Rush Creek Lollipop (page 56)

Rides for Experienced Bikers

These are the best rides for experienced cyclists—either because they are long, they are hilly or they are challenging to follow.

1. Scaling the Heights (page 134)
2. Take the Blaine (page 68)
3. Gateway Trail, full trail (page 80)
4. Trails to Light Rails, 21-mile route (page 38)
5. Gorge-ous Mississippi (page 20)

Iconic Twin Cities Rides

These routes showcase some of the icons of the Twin Cities, from the *Spoonbridge and Cherry* to the downtown riverfronts.

1. Trails to Light Rails (page 38)
2. Gorge-ous Mississippi (page 20)
3. Cedar Lake Express (page 140)
4. Midtown Lollipop (page 26)
5. Samuel Morgan Trail (page 32)

Rides for Nature Lovers

Even though the routes in this book are through Minneapolis and St. Paul, and their surrounding suburbs, the Twin Cities has many natural areas to enjoy. Take one of these routes for a calming ride.

1. Elm Creek Park (page 146)
2. Gateway Trail, the rural segment, after the 55th Street Trailhead (page 80)
3. Rush Creek Lollipop (page 56)
4. Lake Elmo Dumbbell (page 92)
5. Circling the Fort, take the detour down into the state park (page 14)

Bike Route Ratings

Route	Terrain/Hill	Length (in miles)*	Page
Central Metro			
1. Circling the Fort	Intermediate	14	14
2. Gorge-ous Mississippi	Challenging	14 (options: 6, 9 & 12.5)	20
3. Midtown Lollipop	Easy	15 (options: 11.3 & 12.3)	26
4. Samuel Morgan Trail	Intermediate	18 (options: 9.6, 15 & 22)	32
5. Trails to Light Rails	Challenging	21 (options: 8 & 13)	38
Northern Metro			
6. Coon Rapids Dam	Easy	15 (options: 4, 13 & 15+)	44
7. Rice Creek West	Intermediate	11 (option: 8.2)	50
8. Rush Creek Lollipop	Easy	18 (option: shorten, 14 & 18+)	56
9. Slow & Steady	Easy	15 (options: 8.5, 9.5 & 12)	62
10. Take the Blaine	Easy	18 (option: 4)	68
11. Trails to Rails	Intermediate	15	74
Eastern Metro			
12. Gateway Trail	Intermediate	36 (options: shorten, 14.3 & 18.5)	80
13. Groovin' the Grove	Intermediate	11 (option: 9.2)	86
14. Lake Elmo Dumbbell	Easy	15 (option: 10)	92
15. Phalen Inside & Out	Intermediate	13 (options: 3, 8.3 & 13+)	98
16. Woodbury Wander	Intermediate	15 (options: 12 & 15.5)	104
Southern Metro			
17. Around the Zoo	Intermediate	15 (options: 9.8, 10.2, 13.2 & 16)	110
18. Bet the Farm	Intermediate	16	116
19. Highline Highlights	Challenging	14	122
20. Concord by the Mississippi	Easy	12 (easily shortened)	128
21. Scaling the Heights	Challenging	13.5 (options: 11.9, 12.5 & 12.9)	134
Western Metro			
22. Cedar Lake Express	Easy	14 (option: 5.5 & 14+)	140
23. Elm Creek Park	Intermediate	15 (options: 5 & 7.5)	146
24. Good Medicine	Intermediate	15 (option: 7.5 & 15+)	152
25. Purgatory in Eden	Challenging	14 (options: 6, 13 & 14+)	158

* most routes also have options to lengthen them

Overview Map

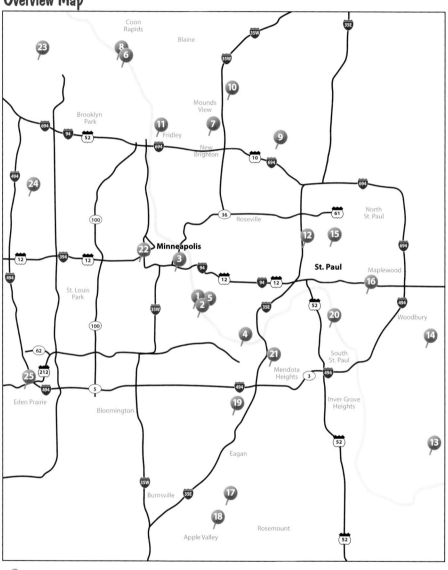

marker represents each route's starting point

Spectacular views of the junction of the Mississippi and Minnesota Rivers

Why Jon Recommends this Ride: Boasting a commanding view of the surrounding valleys, Fort Snelling was built in the early 1820s at the strategic confluence of the Minnesota and Mississippi Rivers. The views remain today and taking a ride around the river junction is still a great strategy.

Tips: Minnehaha Park has a pay parking lot, but there is ample free parking on nearby streets.

This route has no regular rest area, but does have several good spots to take a break, which are outlined in the Points of Interest section on page 18.

Length: 14 miles

Location: Minneapolis, St. Paul, Lilydale, Mendota Heights, Mendota and Ft. Snelling

Terrain: Mostly rolling terrain and steady grades with one steep descent.

Considerations:

There are a couple of tricky turns on this route. Keep a close eye on the route directions, especially as you pass through Fort Snelling.

There are a few sections of Mississippi River Blvd., where the trail is a narrow combined bike and pedestrian path. Use caution here. More-athletic riders might prefer to ride in the bike lane in the street, rather than use the path.

Start Location ⭑: Minnehaha Park, 4801 Minnehaha Ave., Minneapolis,

55417. One of the oldest and most popular parks in Minneapolis, showcasing the 53-foot-high Minnehaha Falls and surrounding limestone bluffs. Amenities at the ride start include parking (see Tips) restrooms, bike rentals, drinking fountains and picnic facilities.

Connecting Routes in this Book:

Trails to Light Rails (page 38) shares a start location.

Gorge-ous Mississippi (page 20) shares a start location.

Samuel Morgan Trail (page 32) crosses this route.

Scaling the Heights (page 134) shares a segment.

Route Options:

- For a more scenic but challenging route through Fort Snelling, turn right at the end of the Mendota Bridge and take the steep trail down into the state park, then climb back up the river bluff to the south end of Minnehaha Park.

- When the site is open for visitors, starting and ending the ride at Historic Fort Snelling can be a great option.

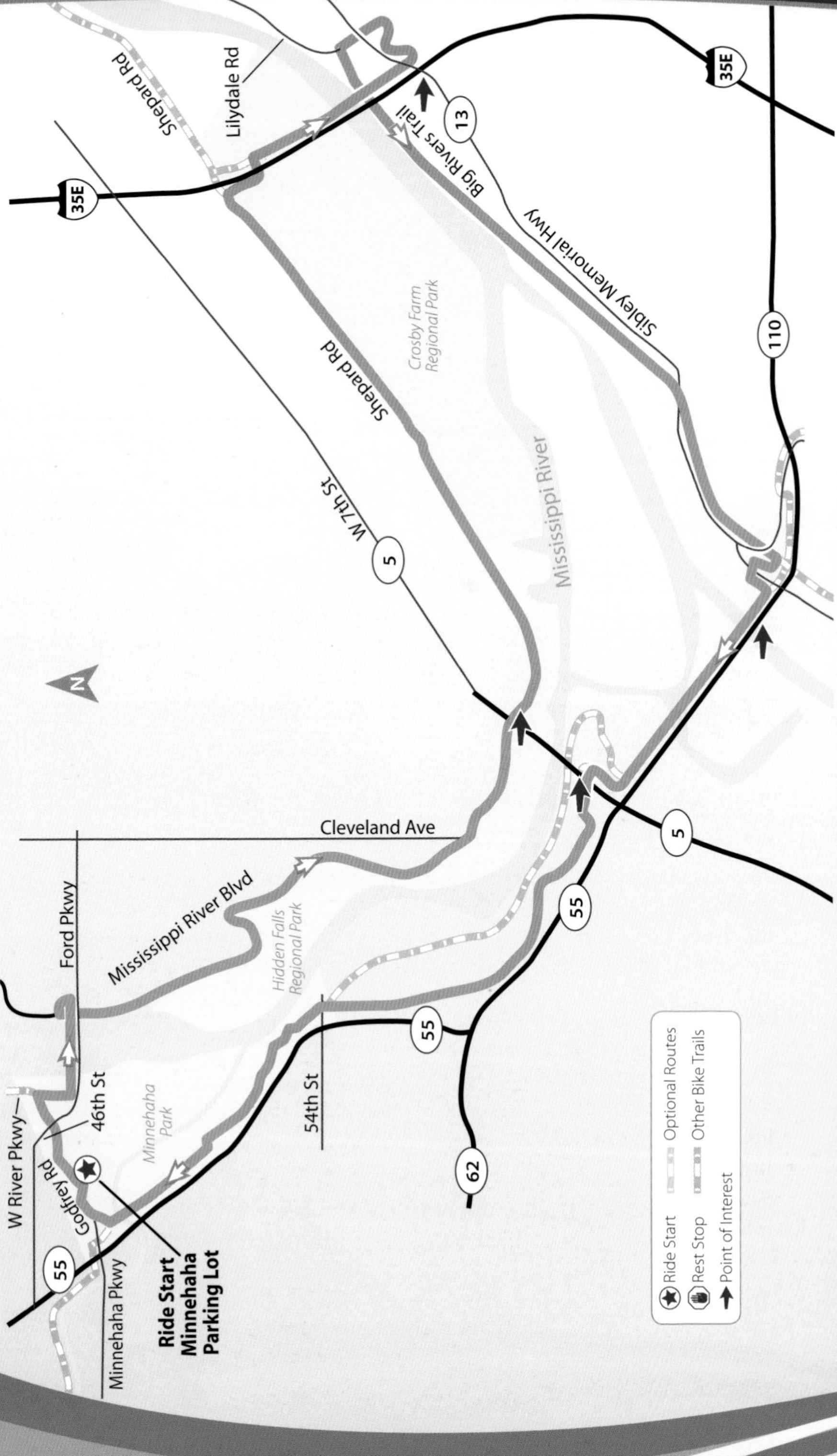

Lilydale Rd

Shepard Rd

35E

Big Rivers Trail

13

Crosby Farm Regional Park

Sibley Memorial Hwy

35E

110

Shepard Rd

W 7th St

5

Mississippi River

N

Cleveland Ave

Ford Pkwy

Mississippi River Blvd

Hidden Falls Regional Park

5

55

55

46th St

Goodrich Rd

W River Pkwy

Minnehaha Park

54th St

55

62

Minnehaha Pkwy

Ride Start Minnehaha Parking Lot

★ Ride Start	Optional Routes
☕ Rest Stop	Other Bike Trails
↑ Point of Interest	

Step by Step Directions:

- **Watch for this turn:** From Minnehaha Park, ride east along Godfrey Rd. toward the Mississippi. After crossing under 46th St., and shortly before the parkway curves left to become West River Pkwy., you will see a trail exiting on your right.

- Turn right onto the trail and follow it up to the Ford Bridge. Turn left to take the bridge across the Mississippi.

- At the east end of the bridge, follow the sidewalk around to the left, then cross Mississippi River Blvd. and turn left onto the adjacent bike trail.

- Follow Mississippi River Blvd. for just over 2 miles to the Hwy. 5 bridge. Just after the trail crosses over Hwy. 5, you will see the beautiful Two Rivers Junction Overlook on your right. The overlook offers a spectacular view of the river valleys and features a stone inlay map of the area around the confluence. Though early in the ride, this is a great place to stop to get a drink of water and take in the view.

- As you leave the overlook, follow the frontage road for about a quarter mile, then jog across the road to follow the upper trail that parallels Shepard Rd. (Note: The lower trail will take you down into Crosby Farm Park and the start location for the Samuel Morgan Trail, page 32.)

- Follow Shepard Rd. to the I-35E overpass. Turn right to follow the trail along the entrance ramp, then through the tunnel under I-35E. Upon exiting the tunnel, turn right to follow the bridge across the Mississippi River.

- After crossing the Mississippi, the trail will climb up to Hwy. 13. When you reach Hwy. 13, turn right and follow the path for a short block before turning right again to follow the curving Lilydale Rd. down the hill toward the river. If you want a snack or a mid-ride pit stop, you can take a small detour here to the Holiday Station store on Hwy. 13. Instead of turning right on 13, cross the highway, then turn left to follow the bridge over I-35E to the convenience store.

- At the bottom of the hill, just before passing under the old wooden railroad bridge, turn left onto the Big Rivers Trail.

- Follow the Big Rivers Trail for 2.5 miles, through the tiny town of Mendota. Just past Mendota, the trail passes through a tunnel. Just past the tunnel, take a sharp right to exit the trail, then double back to get onto the Mendota Bridge for one more river crossing.

- **Watch for these turns:** The Mendota Bridge brings you across to Fort Snelling. As you come off the bridge, stay left, then take your first left to ride through the parking lot for the Historic Fort.

- On the far side of the parking lot, stay right and follow the driveway to the frontage road. Turn right onto the bike trail, which parallels Hwy. 55 back toward Minnehaha Park. After three-quarters of a mile, the trail empties out onto a short, nearly unused street called Minnehaha Park Dr. Continue in the street for a long block to reach the southern edge of Minnehaha Park.

- The bike trail through Minnehaha Park jogs back and forth across Minnehaha Dr. a couple of times before passing the historic Minnehaha Depot, across the street from the main pavilion and parking area.

Points of Interest ➡ : Two Rivers Overlook (mile 3.0) has a drinking
fountain, benches and a beautiful view of the valley. The overlook itself is laid out as a map of the area, showing both rivers, Pike Island, and the surrounding communities.

There is a Holiday Station Store (near mile 5.9), which makes a convenient stop if you need a restroom or a quick snack. It is located just west of the route on Hwy. 13. After coming across the river on the I-35E bridge, cross Hwy. 13, turn left onto the sidewalk and cross back over I-35E.

The Mendota Bridge (mile 9.2) is one of the few spots in the metro area that offers a view of both the Minneapolis and St. Paul downtown skyline. It also overlooks Fort Snelling State Park.

When open, the Historic Fort Snelling Visitor Center (mile 10) offers restrooms and drinking fountains.

Extended Activities:

- Minnehaha Park (ride start) is a great place to spend a summer day with the family. It offers picnic grounds, several miles of walking trails, and views of the beautiful Minnehaha Falls. If you're hungry, the Sea Salt Eatery is open seasonally. Located in the main pavilion, it specializes in simple seafood fare. They also serve ice cream and cookies as well as wine and beer. There are also several chain restaurants just north of the park, along Hiawatha Ave.

- Historic Fort Snelling (mile 10) is a "living history" museum where actors reenact the everyday life of the settlers, soldiers and American Indians who called this area home in the 1800s. The fort was built in the 1820s and saw continuous use as a military post for over 100 years. It was retired in 1946 and declared a National Historic Landmark in 1960.

- Fort Snelling State Park (mile 10 on the alternate route) is the only state park located right in the Twin Cities. It offers canoeing, wildlife viewing, swimming, and hiking trails. The visitor center offers exhibits about the history and natural resources of the area. The park is a kind of urban oasis and hosts a remarkable abundance of wildlife just a few miles from the skylines of Minneapolis and St. Paul. While at the park, I have spotted fox, otters and deer near the bike trails and once had a coyote run across the trail in front of me. This is a fine place for any nature-lover to linger.

Jon's Notes: I have been riding along the rivers and around Fort Snelling since I was 6 years old, but many of the connections that make this route possible are quite new. When I was growing up, the trail along Shepard Rd. was possibly the worst bike trail in the Twin Cities. Today, it is one of the best. The trail across I-35E is another recent addition to the metro area's fine bikeways, as is the trail across the Mendota Bridge.

Until recently, the Mendota Bridge was simply unfit for bicycles. It sported a sidewalk that was too narrow in some places for a bicycle to pass through. On rare occasions, however, when the wind was right and we were feeling spunky, my bike-racing club would ride across the bridge with the traffic. This was certainly a very bad idea, but the views from the bridge were spectacular. Today you can safely enjoy these views from the bridge's new bike trail. While the traffic is noisy, riders are now comfortably separated from the highway by a four-foot-high concrete barrier.

Circling the Fort Trail Environment

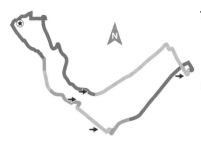

The "feel" of this route
YELLOW—urban areas or along busy streets
BLUE—suburban areas or neighborhoods
GREEN—parks, parkways and rural or natural settings

GPS Coordinates
- ✪ Start/End (Minnehaha Park): 44° 55' 2.25" N 93° 12' 42.06" W
- ➜ Point of Interest (Two Rivers Overlook): 44° 53' 44.72" N   93° 10' 43.03" W
- ➜ Point of Interest (Holiday Station): 44° 53' 59.60" N   93° 8' 13.30" W
- ➜ Point of Interest (Mendota Bridge): 44° 53' 5.70" N   93° 10' 22.96" W
- ➜ Point of Interest (Fort Snelling): 44° 53' 33.63" N   93° 10' 57.87" W

Follow the bluffs overlooking the Mississippi River from Minnehaha to St. Anthony Falls

Why Jon Recommends this Ride: Along its entire 2,530-mile length, the Mississippi River passes through just one true gorge, which runs from St. Anthony Falls to the area near Minnehaha Creek. For most of this distance, the Mighty Mississippi is a ribbon of green that snakes through the cities, flanked by parkways and bicycle trails. With few cross streets, several different mileage options, lots of connecting routes, and the limestone and sandstone bluffs of the Mississippi almost constantly in view, this is a ride you will come back to again and again.

Tips: Minnehaha Park has a pay parking lot, but there is ample free parking on nearby streets.

You can avoid riding on University Ave. at mile 7.4 by cutting through the parking lot behind Stanford Hall, a U of M dormitory. Turn right into the parking lot and follow it through to the pedestrian bridge over the railroad trench. You can take the bridge (though it is in poor shape), or follow the sidewalk to 14th Ave.

Length: 14 miles, with options of 6 miles, 9 miles and 12.5 miles

Location: Minneapolis, St. Paul

Terrain: Mostly flat to rolling terrain with two long, fairly steep hills.

Considerations: There are two long, steep hills along the River Road, one on each side of the river.

Start Location ⭐: Minnehaha Park, 4801 Minnehaha Ave., Minneapolis, 55417. One of the oldest and most popular parks in Minneapolis, Minnehaha park showcases the 53-foot-high Minnehaha Falls and surrounding limestone bluffs. Amenities at the ride start include parking (see Tips), restrooms, the Sea Salt Eatery, bike rentals, drinking fountains and picnic facilities. There are also several chain restaurants just north of the park, along Hiawatha Ave.

Connecting Routes in this Book:

Trails to Light Rails (page 38) shares the start location and a long segment.

Midtown Lollipop (page 26) shares a segment.

Circling the Fort (page 14) shares the start location and a very short segment.

Route Options: It is possible to avoid the steep hill on East River Road at mile 8.0 by cutting through the U of M campus. After turning onto campus on 14th Ave., turn left onto Pillsbury Dr. SE. Follow Pillsbury through campus (it jogs left at Church St.), until it becomes Harvard St. Continue on Harvard St. back to East River Pkwy. You can also shorten the ride by crossing the Mississippi at any of the other bridges along the ride:

6 miles Lake St. Bridge (at mile 2.5).

9 miles Franklin Ave. Bridge (at mile 3.9).

12.5 miles Bridge #9 (access from the spur trail at mile 5.5).

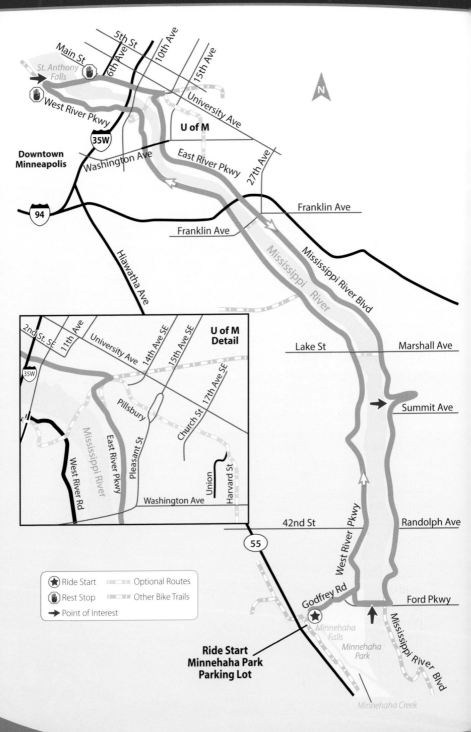

Downtown Minneapolis

U of M

U of M Detail

Ride Start Minnehaha Park Parking Lot

⭐ Ride Start
✋ Rest Stop
➡ Point of Interest

Optional Routes
Other Bike Trails

Step by Step Directions:

- As with two other routes in this book (Trails to Light Rails and Two Rivers Junction), this ride begins at Minnehaha Park.

- From the park, the route heads out to the river and follows the bike trail along West River Pkwy. all the way into downtown Minneapolis. This section of the route is part of the Minneapolis "Grand Rounds" trail system. The trail passes under all of the bridges that cross the river until the trail reaches downtown, meaning that the only cross traffic comes from a handful of parking lots along the river.

- From the start of the route up to the Franklin Ave. Bridge, the route is flat or gently rolling. Near Franklin Ave., however, the trail slopes down the bluff to the river flats about 100' below; it then climbs back up to the top of the gorge as it passes by the striking Guthrie Theater building.

- Just past the Guthrie, the route enters the Historic Mill District and crosses over the river on the beautiful and historic Stone Arch Bridge. Mill City Park, located on the west end of the bridge, is the official rest stop for the ride, but there are other great spots to stop nearby. Hennepin Island Park, located at the east end of the bridge, is a great picnic spot.

Rest Stop 🚻**:** Mill Ruins Park (mile 6.3), 103 Portland Ave. S, Minneapolis, 55401. Hennepin Island Park (mile 6.7) is another option. Amenities at Mill Ruins Park include restrooms, a drinking fountain and sightseeing. For dining options, head just south of Mill Ruins Park and take the wide walkway in between the Mill City Museum and the Guthrie Theater out to 2nd St., where you'll find an assortment of restaurants and cafes. On Saturday mornings in summer and early fall, the walkway is also home to the Mill City Farmers Market. For additional dining options, you can also head north of Hennepin Island Park to St. Anthony Main, which offers an assortment of restaurants along the beautiful cobblestone street.

- There is no connecting bike trail south of Hennepin Island Park. Instead, the route turns right just past the end of the Stone Arch Bridge onto an unnamed service road between the U of M Steam Plant and a newer apartment complex. The road passes under I-35W and 10th St., then parallels a set of railroad tracks a short distance. The road changes from pavement to firm-packed gravel for about a block before connecting to the new Dinkytown Greenway bike trail.

- Turn right on the Dinkytown Greenway and follow it for a block toward Bridge #9. Turn left before the bridge and follow the access road up to East River Pkwy. A short distance along East River Pkwy, a bike trail reappears on the right side of the street, just before dropping down the bluff once again. If you prefer to avoid the hill, you can backtrack on East River Pkwy. to Pillsbury Dr. and cut through the U of M campus instead. Check the inset map for details.

- Whichever way you go, the route then parallels the river road all the way back to the Ford Bridge, where it crosses over the river and returns to Minnehaha Park. The river road is called East River Pkwy. in Minneapolis and Mississippi River Blvd. after crossing into St. Paul, but you may never know the difference because the views are equally beautiful and there is only one significant intersection to navigate the whole way back.

Points of Interest ➔ : The Stone Arch Bridge (mile 6.5) and the Ford Bridge (mile 13.3) offer spectacular views of the Mississippi River and the Locks and Dams that are managed by the Army Corps of Engineers.

There is an attractive overlook where Summit Ave. meets Mississippi River Blvd. (mile 11.5).

Extended Activities:

- Minnehaha Park (ride start). This is a great place to spend a summer day with the family. It offers picnic grounds, several miles of walking trails, and views of the beautiful Minnehaha Falls.

- The Historic Mill District (mile 6.2). Here you can tour icons of Minneapolis history. Meander along the St. Anthony Falls Heritage Trail, which runs through Mill Ruins Park and across the historic Stone Arch Bridge, or tour the Mill City Museum. At Upper St. Anthony Falls Lock and Dam, the Army Corps of Engineers offers free tours that cover the history of the falls, navigation on the Mississippi, and the operation of the lock structure.

Jon's Notes: I grew up less than a mile from the Mississippi River in Minneapolis and have biked these trails more than any others in the book. I took my first trips along the trails overlooking this river gorge when I was about six years old; I struggled to keep up with the rest of my family as I pedaled on my orange single-speed bike with its coaster brake and banana seat. Our rides would take us from our house to the Franklin Ave. Bridge, then along the river to Minnehaha Park or nearby Lake Nokomis for a picnic. Many years later, the river parkways became part of my regular training routes on my morning rides with the St. Paul Bicycle Racing Club. With my racing days long behind me, my rides along the river are once again with family—typically riding a tandem together with my mom.

The Mississippi River gorge is an icon of the Twin Cities. This route showcases the gorge from one end to the other. These trails are some of the oldest bikeways in the metro area and continue to be some of the best. If you like casual riding in the city, these trails are bound to be some of your favorites, as they have been for me for over 35 years.

Gorge-ous Mississippi Trail Environment

The "feel" of this route
YELLOW—urban areas or along busy streets
BLUE—suburban areas or neighborhoods
GREEN—parks, parkways and rural or natural settings

GPS Coordinates
- ✪ Start/End (Minnehaha Park): 44° 55' 2.25" N 93° 12' 42.06" W
- ⦿ Rest Stop (Mill Ruins Park): 44° 58' 40.38" N 93° 15' 5.25" W
- ⦿ Rest Stop (Hennepin Island Park): 44° 58' 52.24" N 93° 15' 2.86" W
- → Point of Interest (Stone Arch Bridge): 44° 58' 50.98" N 93° 15' 31.41" W
- → Point of Interest (Overlook): 44° 56' 29.53" N 93° 11' 52.45" W
- → Point of Interest (Ford Bridge): 44° 55' 4.43" N 93° 12' 4.35" W

Ride the most popular bike trail in the metro to the most popular lake in Minneapolis

Why Jon Recommends this Ride: The Midtown Greenway sees more bicycle traffic than any other trail in Minnesota. Stretching across South Minneapolis from Lake Calhoun to the Mississippi River, it is heavily used by commuters and recreational riders alike. This route follows the western section of the Greenway from Hiawatha Ave. out to Lake Calhoun and Lake of the Isles.

Tips: The route is completely flat and has just a few street crossings, making it one of the best rides in the collection for bike trailers and single-speed bikes.

Length: 15 miles, with options of 11.3 miles, 12.3 miles and 15-plus miles

Location: Minneapolis

Terrain: Completely flat. This is an ideal route for those with bike trailers and single-speed bikes.

Considerations: Be sure to stop at the stop signs along the Midtown Greenway. These are enforced, and bicyclists have been ticketed $125 for failing to stop.

The Greenway is the most heavily used bike trail in the Twin Cities and can become crowded on nice days. Be mindful of other trail users along the route.

Start Location (★): East Phillips Park, 2307 17th Ave. S, Minneapolis, 55404. Located just south of Downtown, East Phillips Park is home to the "greenest" building in the Minneapolis Parks system, the brand new East Phillips Park Cultural and Community Center. Amenities at ride start include parking, indoor restrooms (open evenings and weekend daytimes—check building hours), drinking fountains, a playground, picnic facilities and a wading pool. There is no food at the ride start; however, there are numerous cafes, restaurants and a grocery store located a few blocks away on Franklin Ave.

Connecting Routes in this Book:

Trails to Light Rails (page 38) shares a segment near the midpoint.

Cedar Lake Express (page 140) comes within less than a mile of the Midtown Greenway bike trail.

Gorge-ous Mississippi (page 20) comes within 1.5 miles of this route.

Route Options:

11.3 or 12.3 miles For a shorter ride, skip the loop around Lake Calhoun (cuts off 3.7 miles) or Lake of the Isles (cuts 2.7 miles).

The Midtown Greenway can also be used as a shortcut on the Trails to Light Rails ride (page 38).

15+ miles For a slightly longer ride, take the bike-bridge over Hiawatha at 24th just past the ride start, then follow the Hiawatha Bike Trail south to the Sabo Bridge just north of 28th.

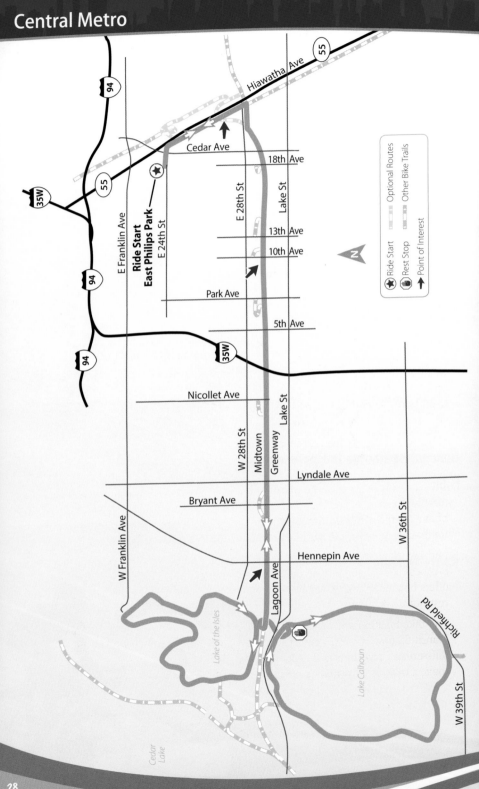

Step by Step Directions:

- Our ride begins and ends at East Phillips Park, less than a mile north of the Greenway. Begin by riding east on 24th St., crossing Cedar Ave., and getting on the path along Hiawatha Ave. Follow this south-southeast to a right turn along 28th St., then jog left to get on the Greenway.

- Once you are on the Greenway, it is a straight shot west to the lakes. There are two lake-loops on this ride, and you can ride them in whatever order you like. My personal preference is to ride around Calhoun first, and then take a break at the Tin Fish before riding around Lake of the Isles. Both lakes are circled clockwise. All of Lake of the Isles and most of Calhoun are also circled by parkways that are fairly bicycle friendly. Faster riders may prefer to ride in the street if the bike paths are crowded.

Rest Stop 🖐: Lake Calhoun Pavilion, the Tin Fish (mile 7.5), 3000 Calhoun Pkwy. E, Minneapolis, 55408. Amenities at rest stop include indoor restrooms, drinking fountains, and picnic tables. If you are planning a long rest stop, the Tin Fish restaurant serves fresh seafood on a patio overlooking Lake Calhoun. They are open every day of the summer from 11 a.m. to 9 p.m. When the weather is nice you can expect a long line and a wait for your food after you order. I have never found it excessive, but some customers report it taking up to an hour. Sometimes there is a shorter line available just for beverage orders, and the drinking fountains are always available.

- After rounding the lakes, the return to East Phillips Park is along the exact same smooth, flat, traffic-free route as the ride out.

Points of Interest ➡ : The Martin Olav Sabo Bridge (mile 0.7) is the architectural highlight of the ride. This beautiful cable-stayed suspension bridge was built as part of the Midtown Greenway, offering bikes and pedestrians a traffic-free route over Hwy. 55.

Midtown Bike Center (mile 1.8 and at mile 13 on the return) is the only business located directly on the Greenway. Run by Freewheel Bike, the center offers bike repair, bike storage, bike rentals, a public shop, a cafe, and public restrooms with showers.

The Bike Fixation self-service repair kiosk (mile 3.7) located in the Uptown Transit Station, directly above the Midtown Greenway, is the world's first self-service bicycle repair kiosk. The kiosk features a bike repair stand with tools; a bicycle air pump; and a vending machine that dispenses spare tubes, patch kits, trail maps, snacks and other bicycle essentials. To get to the kiosk, exit the Greenway using the ramp up to Girard Ave. Cross the bridge, then follow the path into the transit station.

Extended Activities:

- Lake Calhoun, 3000 Calhoun Pkwy. E, Minneapolis, 55408. Lake Calhoun is one of the most popular recreational lakes in the Twin Cities and offers a variety of amenities for visitors. Wheel Fun Rentals offers boat rentals next door to the Tin Fish restaurant. Thomas Beach is located on the south end of Lake Calhoun at mile 5.6. This popular swimming beach and park offers a great view of the downtown skyline.

- The Bakken Museum (mile 6.0), 3537 Zenith Ave., Minneapolis, 55416. Located just off Lake Calhoun, the Bakken is a unique museum that explores electricity and magnetism in nature and medicine. To get there, exit the bike path at 36th St., then turn right on Zenith.

- Midtown Global Market (mile 1.8 and mile 13 on the return), 920 E Lake St., Minneapolis, 55407. Located across the trail from the Midtown Bike Center in the old Sears Building on Lake street, the Midtown Global Market offers a diverse selection of shops, restaurants and delis. This is a fun place to browse for gifts, and a great place to stop for a treat near the end of the ride.

Jon's Notes: The Greenway runs along an old Milwaukee Road railway corridor. The corridor is sunk below street level from Hiawatha Ave. to just past Hennepin Ave., and is accessed by ramps or stairs. There is only one at-grade street-crossing along this segment, making the bulk of this ride completely away from car traffic. Like many metro area cyclists, I began using the Greenway year-round and at all times of the day and night immediately after it opened in 2000. In a dozen years, I have never been alone on the trail. Even commuting home after midnight in the winter I always see at least one other rider. The trail truly is a gem among Twin Cities area bikeways.

Midtown Lollipop Trail Environment

The "feel" of this route

YELLOW—urban areas or along busy streets

BLUE—suburban areas or neighborhoods

GREEN—parks, parkways and rural or natural settings

GPS Coordinates

⊛ Start/End (East Phillips Park): 44° 57' 36.86" N
93° 14' 58.60" W

⊛ Rest Stop (Lake Calhoun Pavilion): 44° 56' 53.22" N   93° 18' 23.02" W

→ Point of Interest (Martin Olav Sabo Bridge): 44° 57' 15.46" N   93° 14' 33.50" W

→ Point of Interest (Midtown Bike Center): 44° 57' 1.52" N   93° 15' 37.02" W

→ Point of Interest (Bike Fixation): 44° 57' 1.07" N   93° 17' 54.70" W

Explore St. Paul's restored riverfront from one of the best new trails in the metro

Why Jon Recommends this Ride: This trail is a new addition to the bikeways of the Twin Cities area. St. Paul has transformed its downtown riverfront in recent years and the Samuel Morgan Trail showcases this redevelopment. This is an out-and-back ride, and the scenery is great in both directions. And if you are looking for a great family outing, consider taking this ride to the Science Museum of Minnesota, which overlooks the river and the trail.

Tips: To avoid needing to cross the street at the I-35E overpass, follow the trail loop toward the river and under the freeway. It's a very short detour, and you don't need to watch out for cars.

Samuel Morgan Trail

Length: 18 miles out-and-back, with options of 9.6 miles, 15 miles and 22 miles

Location: St. Paul

Terrain: Flat or rolling terrain for most of the route, with a steady climb up to the intersection with Otto Ave. The optional segment up the Battle Creek Trail is a long, moderate grade—and a good workout!

Considerations: Some sections of this route are prone to flooding during the spring melt. Spots along the trails in Crosby Farm Park can get covered with silt from Crosby Lake, and the stretch of the Samuel Morgan Trail below Lowertown in downtown St. Paul has been completely submerged in some years. If you ride this route early in the season, check the trail conditions and be ready to shorten the trip.

Start Location ⭐: Crosby Farm Regional Park, 2595 Crosby Farm Rd., St. Paul, 55116. Amenities at ride start include parking, a picnic shelter, restrooms and a drinking fountain.

Connecting Routes in this Book:

Circling the Fort (page 14) shares a segment.

Route Options:

9.6 miles Since this is an out-and-back route, it is very easy to adjust the distance. Upper Landing Park at mile 4.8 is a great turnaround point if you want a shorter ride.

15 miles If you want to skip the rough trails in Crosby Farm Park, you can begin this ride at the parking lot at Shepard Rd. and Elway St., next to the I-35E overpass.

There is an new alternate trail that diverts away from Shepard Rd. at Randolph Ave. (mile 3.4) and reconnects at Upper Landing Park. For a variety of scenery you might take the alternate trail out and the main trail back.

22 miles For a longer ride, extend the ride up the Battle Creek Trail spur. This adds about 4 miles and quite a bit of hill climbing to the ride.

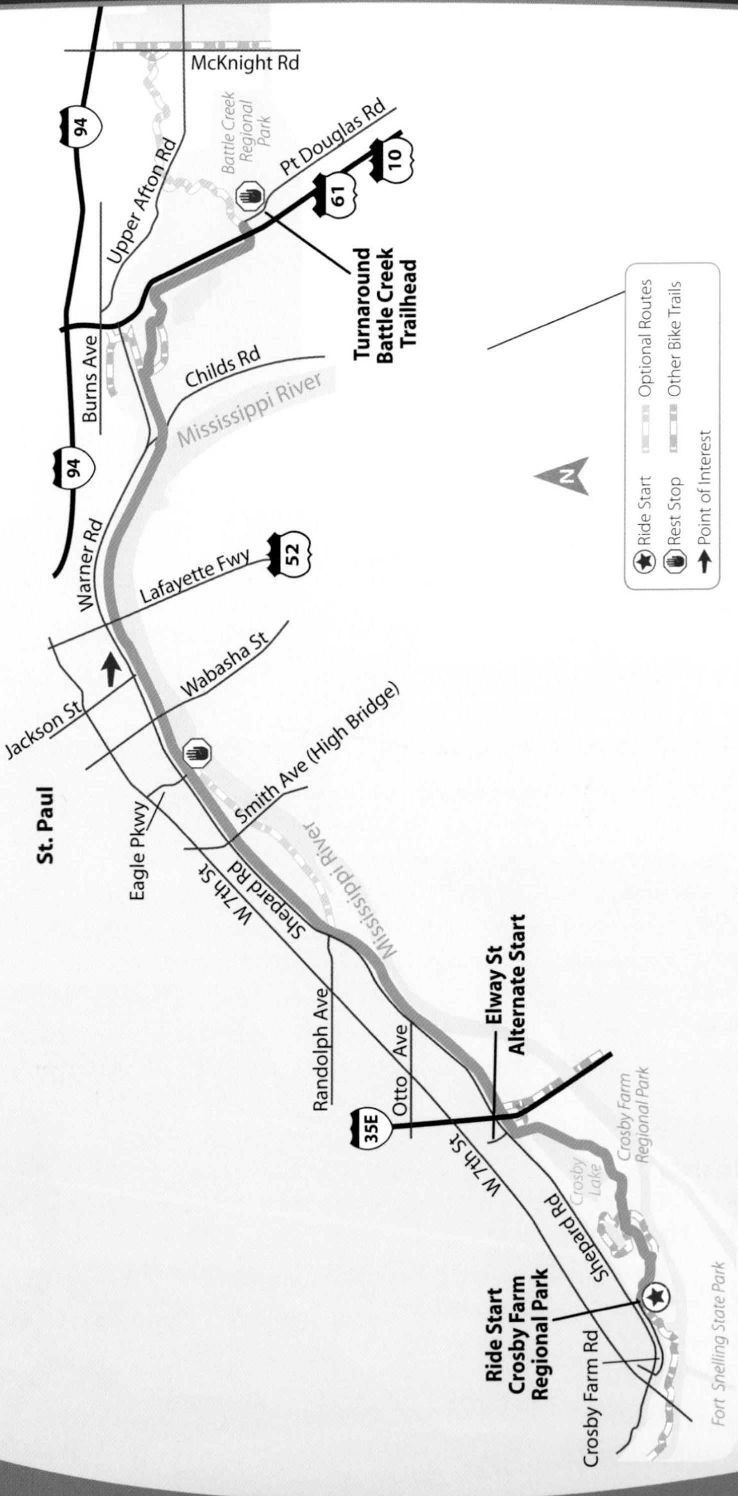

McKnight Rd

94

Upper Afton Rd

Battle Creek Regional Park

Pt Douglas Rd

61

10

**Turnaround
Battle Creek
Trailhead**

Burns Ave

94

Childs Rd

Mississippi River

Warner Rd

Lafayette Fwy

52

Jackson St

Wabasha St

St. Paul

Smith Ave (High Bridge)

Eagle Pkwy

W 7th St

Shepard Rd

Mississippi River

Randolph Ave

Otto Ave

**Elway St
Alternate Start**

Crosby Farm
Regional Park

Crosby Lake

35E

W 7th St

Shepard Rd

Crosby Farm Rd

**Ride Start
Crosby Farm
Regional Park**

Fort Snelling State Park

N

Ride Start
Rest Stop
↑ Point of Interest

Optional Routes
Other Bike Trails

Step by Step Directions:

- The ride begins in the heavily wooded Crosby Farm Park. Begin by following the bike trail east from the main pavilion. There are several trail junctions in the first half mile of the route. Check the map for details. Keep heading east until you end up riding along the southern shore of Crosby Lake.

- The trail exits the Crosby Farm Park and joins the Samuel Morgan Trail at a new parking area just west of the I-35E bridge. Turn right as you exit the park and follow the trail under the I-35E bridge. If you want to avoid the traffic lights and street crossings here, you can make a small detour to the right to go through a tunnel under the freeway.

- The next few miles of the Samuel Morgan Trail are rolling terrain, with a small, but steep, hill coming at mile 2.5. Conveniently, there is a drinking fountain located right at the top of that climb!

- A mile farther on, at the intersection with Randolph Ave., the trail splits. The lower trail is newer and follows along the river. The upper trail continues along Shepard Rd. Both are nice trails, and both take you right to the rest stop at Upper Landing Park.

Rest Stop(🖐): Upper Landing Park (mile 4.8). Shepard Rd. and Chestnut St., St. Paul, 55102. Amenities at the rest stop include benches and a drinking fountain. There is no food right at the park, but the Seven Corners area of downtown St. Paul is just 2 blocks up the hill.

- From Upper Landing Park, the trail continues along the downtown waterfront, just a few feet from the river. This section of the trail is prone to flooding in the springtime, and may be closed if the river is running high.

- At the eastern edge of downtown, the river bends south and the road—now called Warner Rd.—curves away from it to the east before rising up onto a bridge over the railroad lines.

- **Watch for this turn:** Shortly after the overpass, and just before Warner Rd. climbs up a steep hill, turn right onto a trail that leads into a small patch of woods and wetlands.

- The trail splits just south of Warner Rd. You can follow either trail, as they join back together after a quarter mile. The trail emerges from the woods along Hwy. 61 and follows it south for a little less than a mile before ducking under the highway and arriving at the Battle Creek Trail and picnic area parking lot, the turnaround point for the main route.

Turnaround Point: Battle Creek Park Trail and picnic area (mile 9.0). It is located one half mile north of Lower Afton Rd. on Pt. Douglas Rd. S, St. Paul, 55119.

- The Battle Creek Trail and picnic area is located on the edge of the Mississippi River floodplain. The trail to the east is a steady climb up along the creek valley. This is the main turnaround point for the ride and serves as a convenient second rest stop. Be aware that there are no amenities here. However, the creek and the limestone gorge that it has carved are beautiful attractions.

- If you are up for a challenge, I highly recommend continuing east along the Battle Creek Trail. It is about two miles long, and climbs almost 200 feet through the valley carved by Battle Creek.

- From the turnaround point, return to Crosby Farm Park along the same route.

Point of Interest →: The Samuel Morgan Trail passes through Lambert's Landing (mile 5.6), just east of Upper Landing Park. Before the Army Corps of Engineers developed the current lock and dam system, Lambert's Landing was the last point on the Mississippi easily accessible by barge. St. Paul's historic Lowertown District, with its warehouses and railway junctions, grew up around the landing. Even today, the old rail lines and barge ports are a fixture of the St. Paul waterfront.

Extended Activities:

- Science Museum of Minnesota, 120 Kellogg Blvd. W, St. Paul, 55102. My parents often took me to the Science Museum when I was young, but we never rode our bikes there. The old museum was nestled in the middle of downtown, far away from any good family bike route. How things have changed! The beautiful new museum overlooks the Mississippi River and is right across the street from Upper Landing Park. The entrance to the museum is located on Kellogg Blvd. To get there, follow the sidewalk on the east side of Eagle Pkwy. up to Kellogg, turn right, and proceed to the museum's entrance.

Jon's Notes: When I was growing up, I considered the downtown St. Paul riverfront a place to avoid—especially when biking. The area felt industrial and the trail that ran along Shepard Rd. was little more than a narrow sidewalk with heaving pavement. Today, things are different! The newly reconstructed Samuel Morgan Regional Trail is now one of the best bikeways in the metro area. The trail is wide and smooth, has minimal cross traffic, and offers great views of the river. Shepard Rd. and the riverfront have seen substantial upgrades as well. The revitalized riverfront now boasts parks, housing developments, and the backyard of the Science Museum of Minnesota. Today, the Samuel Morgan Trail gets substantial year-round use from recreational cyclists and bike commuters alike.

The trails in Crosby Farm Park, by contrast, have seen some better days, but the rough surface is a small price to pay for the scenery. In addition to the river and two small undeveloped lakes, you are likely to see some wildlife. On several occasions I have had a chipmunk dash across the path in front of me, and on my last ride through the park, I spotted a Baltimore oriole along the trail.

Samuel Morgan Trail Environment

The "feel" of this route

YELLOW—urban areas or along busy streets

BLUE—suburban areas or neighborhoods

GREEN—parks, parkways and rural or natural settings

GPS Coordinates

⊛ Start/End (Crosby Farm Park): 44° 53' 51.78" N 93° 9' 56.32" W

⊚ Rest Stop (Upper Landing Park): 44° 56' 27.29" N   93° 5' 55.68" W

⊚ Turnaround/Rest Stop (Battle Creek Park): 44° 56' 6.89" N   93° 1' 43.75" W

→ Point of Interest (Lambert's Landing): 44° 56' 47.69" N   93° 4' 57.59" W

Follow the parkways around south Minneapolis and return along the river or by light rail

Why Jon Recommends this Ride:
This is an urban ride, and cuts through the center of downtown Minneapolis, but it hardly feels like one. The ride follows parkways along lakes and creeks, and there are surprisingly few cross streets for a city ride. From downtown you can either ride back to the start along the Mississippi River, or you can take the light rail. Either way, you will get to see some of the finest greenways Minneapolis has to offer.

Tips:
Minnehaha Park has a pay parking lot, but there is ample free parking on nearby streets.

When you return to the park on the light rail, get off at the 46th St. Station and follow the bike path next to the tracks south to the park.

Get information on how to bring your bike on the light rail here: http://metrotransit.org/bike-n-ride-on-hiawatha-light-rail.aspx

Length: 13 or 21 miles, with an 8-mile option

Location: Minneapolis

Terrain: The 13-mile route is mostly flat, with one short but steep slope where the trail crosses Lyndale Ave. The 21-mile route adds a long climb along the river bluff.

Considerations: Be mindful of the broken pavement at mile 4.25, where the trail crosses over Minnehaha Creek. Around Lake Calhoun, there are also long cracks in the asphalt; these are usually well marked with paint.

On the 21-mile route, there is one substantial hill at mile 17.

The trails around the lakes are popular in the summer and sometimes get quite congested.

Start Location ⭐: Minnehaha Park, 4801 Minnehaha Ave., Minneapolis, 55417. One of the oldest and most popular parks in Minneapolis, this park showcases the 53-foot-high Minnehaha Falls and the surrounding limestone bluffs. Amenities at the ride start include parking (see Tips), restrooms, bike rentals, drinking fountains, and picnic facilities. The Sea Salt Eatery is located in the main park pavilion and there are several chain restaurants just north of the park, along Hiawatha Ave.

Connecting Routes in this Book:

Gorge-ous Mississippi (page 20) has the same start location and shares one long segment.

Cedar Lake Express (page 140) shares a short segment.

Circling the Fort (page 14) has the same start location.

Trails to Rails (page 74) shares a segment.

Midtown Lollipop (page 26) shares a segment.

Route Options:

8 miles For a shorter, 8-mile route, ride the final segment of the 21-mile route backwards, then return to Minnehaha on the light rail.

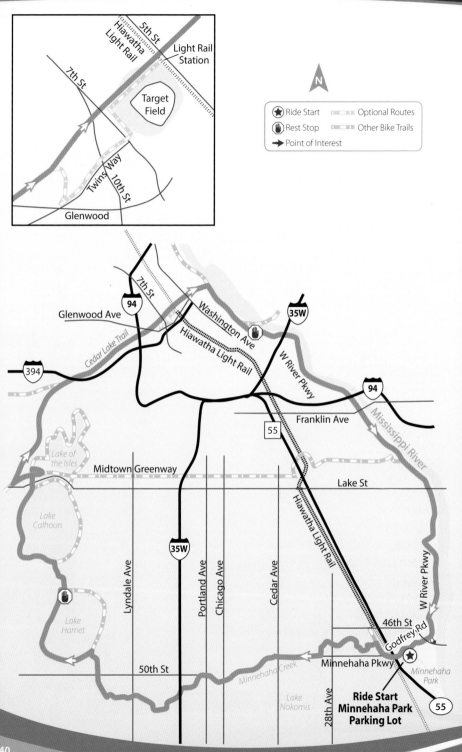

Ride Start
Rest Stop
Point of Interest
Optional Routes
Other Bike Trails

Target Field

5th St
Hiawatha Light Rail
7th St
Light Rail Station
Twins Way
10th St
Glenwood

N

7th St
94
Glenwood Ave
Washington Ave
Hiawatha Light Rail
Cedar Lake Trail
394
35W
W River Pkwy
Franklin Ave
55
94
Mississippi River
Lake of the Isles
Midtown Greenway
Lake St
Lake Calhoun
35W
Lyndale Ave
Portland Ave
Chicago Ave
Cedar Ave
Hiawatha Light Rail
W River Pkwy
Lake Harriet
50th St
Minnehaha Creek
46th St
Godfrey Rd
Minnehaha Pkwy
Minnehaha Park
28th Ave
Lake Nokomis
Ride Start Minnehaha Park Parking Lot
55

Step by Step Directions:

- Begin this ride from the northwest corner of Minnehaha Park. There is a traffic circle at the intersection of Minnehaha Pkwy. and Minnehaha Ave. Follow the bike trails around the traffic circle to the northwest corner, then follow the trail over Hwy. 55 and the light rail line.

- Just past the bridge over the light rail, turn right onto the trail paralleling the tracks. Follow this trail north for about 400 yards, then turn left to follow the trail along Minnehaha Creek.

- Continue along the creek toward Lake Hiawatha, then follow the trail as it curves south toward Lake Nokomis. Cross over Minnehaha Pkwy. near the Lake Nokomis Park building and turn right to follow the trail along the parkway.

- Minnehaha Pkwy. curves south at its intersection with 50th St. Cross over Minnehaha Pkwy. and turn left to continue on the adjacent bike path.

- The trail continues along Minnehaha Creek for another 2 miles before curving north, crossing 50th St. and passing through Lynnhurst Park. At the north end of Lynnhurst, the trail disappears and is replaced by a two-way bike lane that takes you the final two blocks to Lake Harriet.

- At Lake Harriet, cut across the parkway and turn left onto the bike trail to circle the lake clockwise. At the north end of the lake you will find the first rest stop at the Lake Harriet Bandshell.

Rest Stop 1 ✋: Lake Harriet Bandshell (mile 7), 4135 W Lake Harriet Parkway, Minneapolis, 55419. Amenities at the rest stop include restrooms, drinking fountains, food and concessions, and picnic facilities. The Bread and Pickle restaurant is located at Lake Harriet, next to the bandshell. It offers beverages, breakfasts, sandwiches and snacks, including local and sustainably grown food.

- As you leave Lake Harriet, circle around the seating area for the bandshell, then turn left to follow the bike path north toward Lake Calhoun. When you reach Lake Calhoun, turn left to again circle the lake clockwise.

- Near the northwest corner of Calhoun, the trail divides. Stay to the left here and follow the trail along the parkway out to Lake St. Cross Lake St. and continue north for a bit more than one block to the old railroad overpass that carries the Midtown Greenway.

- Immediately after riding under the overpass, make a sharp right turn onto the ramp, then turn right again onto the Midtown Greenway. Follow the Greenway for just under half a mile and take another sharp right onto the Kenilworth Trail.

- Follow the Kennilworth Trail north until it merges with the Cedar Lake Trail, which brings you into Downtown. The 13-mile route ends here, exiting the trail and circling around Target Field to catch the light rail back to Minnehaha Park. Follow the map inset for detailed directions to the light rail platform.

- The 21-mile route continues east on the Cedar Lake Trail until the trail ends at West River Pkwy. Cross over West River Pkwy., then turn right to follow the adjacent trail south about a half mile to Mill Ruins Park, the second rest stop on the ride.

Rest Stop 2(✋)**:** Mill Ruins Park (mile 14.5), 103 Portland Ave. S, Minneapolis, 55401. Mill Ruins Park showcases the history of Minneapolis as a river town. Take a few moments while you are here to ride out onto the Stone Arch Bridge and enjoy the sight of St. Anthony Falls and the old mill ruins that mark the birthplace of the city. Amenities at the rest stop include restrooms, a drinking fountain and sightseeing. If you're looking for a snack, head just south of the park and take the wide walkway in between the Mill City Museum and the Guthrie Theater out to 2nd St. to find an assortment of restaurants and cafes. On Saturday mornings in the summer and early fall, the walkway is also home to the Mill City Farmers Market.

- From Mill Ruins Park it is a straight shot back to Minnehaha Park on the trail along West River Pkwy. Save some energy for the long climb up the river bluff near the Franklin Ave. Bridge, and enjoy the beauty of the river. When you get back to Minnehaha Park, consider making a final "rest stop" at the Sea Salt Eatery. In addition to seafood, their menu includes such refreshments as ice cream and cold beer.

Extended Activities:

- Minnehaha Park (ride start): Minnehaha Park is a great place to spend a summer day with family. It offers picnic grounds, several miles of walking trails, and views of beautiful Minnehaha Falls and the nearby limestone bluffs.

- Lake Harriet (mile 7): The midway point on the 13-mile route, Lake Harriet offers a great variety of recreational activities. Wheel Fun Rentals rents canoes, kayaks and paddleboats by the hour, and the north beach features a buoyed swim area and a floating dock. Another swimming beach is located just a mile farther along the route, at the south end of Lake Calhoun. The historic Como-Harriet Streetcar line runs between Lake Harriet and Lake Calhoun. Board at the Linden Hills Station located at Queen Ave. and 42nd St., just west of the bandshell.

- Target Field (mile 13): Avoid the traffic by riding your bike to a Twins game! Target Field features hundreds of bike parking spaces along its promenade.
- Historic Mill District and Upper St. Anthony Falls Lock and Dam (mile 14): Tour icons of the milling history of Minneapolis. Meander along the St. Anthony Falls Heritage Trail, which runs through Mill Ruins Park and across the historic Stone Arch Bridge, or tour the Mill City Museum. The Army Corps of Engineers also offers free tours of the lock and dam structure.

Jon's Notes: My earliest memories of family bike rides were on these very trails along the river, Minnehaha Creek and the Chain of Lakes. I can still remember riding along Minnehaha Creek on my orange banana-seat bicycle, trying to keep up with my mom and brother on their fancy three-speeds. For a seven-year-old, it was a long ride, but I never turned down the chance to go swimming at the lake.

Trails to Light Rails Trail Environment

The "feel" of this route
YELLOW—urban areas or along busy streets
BLUE—suburban areas or neighborhoods
GREEN—parks, parkways and rural or natural settings

GPS Coordinates
- Start/End (Minnehaha Park): 44° 55' 2.25" N   93° 12' 42.06" W
- Rest Stop (Lake Harriet Bandshell): 44° 55' 43.69" N 93° 18' 30.06" W
- Rest Stop (Mill Ruins Park): 44° 58' 40.38" N   93° 15' 5.25" W

Development and nature intermix, culminating at the stunning Coon Rapids Dam

Why Jon Recommends this Ride: Coon Rapids Dam Regional Park spans the Mississippi River in the north metro, and it is both the starting point and a centerpiece of this ride. The dam itself is an impressive structure that show-cases the power of the often placid-looking Mississippi. The ride mostly winds through Brooklyn Park, with short jaunts into Brooklyn Center and Coon Rapids, and it makes use of the excellent Rush Creek Trail and the bike path along West River Rd., in addition to a number of local trails. The route is one of the flattest in this book, making it a fine choice for those who would prefer to avoid hills.

Tips: While there is a charge to park at the East Visitor Center, parking at the West Visitor Center is free.

Length: 15 miles, with optional routes of 4 miles, 13 miles and 15 miles-plus

Location: Brooklyn Park, Brooklyn Center, Coon Rapids

Terrain: Generally flat with no significant hills.

Considerations: While the parks are gorgeous to bike through, some of the connecting parts of this route are along busy streets (such as Noble Ave.) with numerous stoplights. The route also crosses a highway exit ramp. Parents should consider their children's skills before embarking on this route.

There is an easy-to-miss turn at mile 4.2, just before the route turns south at Xerxes. Keep a close eye out for that one.

A few sections of trail along 70th Ave. (near mile 8.5) are rough and poorly maintained.

Start Location ⭐: Coon Rapids Dam Regional Park West Visitor Center, 10360 West River Rd., Brooklyn Park, 55444. Amenities here include parking (see Tips), restrooms, drinking fountains, concessions, a nature center, picnic facilities, and public art. The East Visitor Center offers bike rentals for use within the park.

Connecting Routes in this Book:

Rush Creek Lollipop (page 56) shares this start location and a short segment of the ride.

Trails to Rails (page 74) comes within 1 mile of this route, along West River Rd.

Route Options:

4 miles Follow the trail along West River Rd. south to Hwy. 610. After crossing Hwy. 610, turn right to join the main route, then cross the bridge and return on the east side of the river.

13 miles Continue on the trail along West River Rd. on the west side of the river, instead of crossing Hwy. 610 at mile 12.7.

15 miles-plus To extend the ride, continue out and back along the Rush Creek Trail or ride out and back on the southbound bike trail along West River Rd.

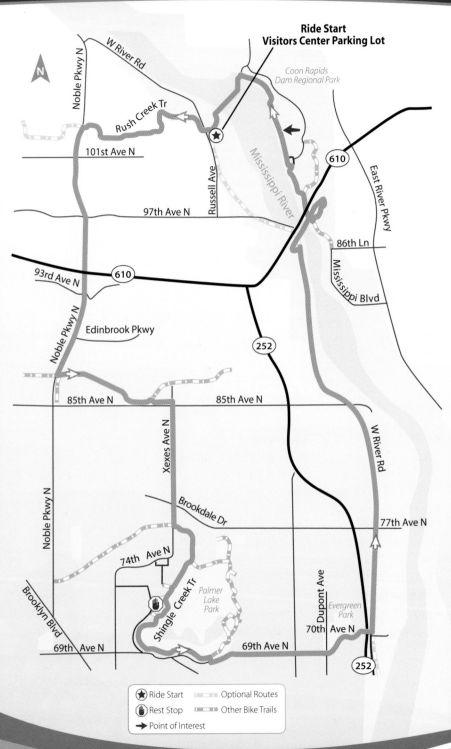

**Ride Start
Visitors Center Parking Lot**

Coon Rapids
Dam Regional Park

N

Noble Pkwy N

W River Rd

Rush Creek Tr

101st Ave N

Russell Ave

Mississippi River

610

East River Pkwy

97th Ave N

86th Ln

Mississippi Blvd

93rd Ave N

610

Noble Pkwy N

Edinbrook Pkwy

252

85th Ave N

85th Ave N

Xexes Ave N

W River Rd

Brookdale Dr

77th Ave N

74th Ave N

Shingle Creek Tr

Palmer
Lake
Park

Dupont Ave

Evergreen
Park

70th Ave N

Brooklyn Blvd

69th Ave N

69th Ave N

252

⭐ Ride Start   ▭▭▭ Optional Routes
✋ Rest Stop   ▭▭▭ Other Bike Trails
➤ Point of Interest

Step by Step Directions:

- From the West Visitor Center, exit the park and cross West River Rd. to pick up the Rush Creek Trail. Follow the Rush Creek Trail for about 1.3 miles to its junction with Noble Pkwy.

- The Rush Creek Trail passes under Noble Pkwy. without intersecting it. Before the tunnel, watch for the branch off of the trail on the left-hand side that takes you up to street level. Turn left (south) onto Shingle Creek Regional Trail, which runs along Noble Pkwy. and follow it about 2.25 miles.

- **Watch for this turn:** Shortly after crossing Kilbirnie Terr., you will turn left to stay on Shingle Creek Trail, leaving Noble Pkwy. The trail entrance is un-marked, but is easy to spot if you are looking for it. It is the only intersecting bike trail along this section of Noble Pkwy., and it is located across the street from a Church of Jesus Christ of Latter-day Saints.

- **Watch for this turn:** Follow Shingle Creek Trail east for about a mile. The trail passes by the backyards of several homes before emerging close to 85th Ave. Shortly after it does, make a right turn onto a nondescript, unmarked connecting trail that will take you out to Xerxes Ave. This is an easy trail junction to miss. If you find yourself riding north again, away from 85th Ave., you have overshot it.

- At the end of the short spur trail, cross Xerxes, then 85th St. to continue south. The trail along this section of Xerxes is concrete and has the feel of a wide sidewalk.

- Just past Brookdale Dr., turn left off of Xerxes and onto the bike trails through Palmer Lake Park. A right turn at the first trail junction in the park and then a left turn at the next trail junction brings you to the rest stop at West Palmer Park.

Rest Stop (🖐): West Palmer Park (mile 6.4), 7110 Palmer Lake Dr., Brooklyn Center, 55429. This park has restrooms, drinking fountains, playground equipment, and a picnic shelter.

- **Watch for this turn:** From the rest stop, the route continues to circle Palmer Lake Park. Near the park's southeast corner, turn right to cross 69th Ave., then turn left to follow the local trail along 69th Ave. east.

- After about a mile, the trail jogs back across 69th at Dupont Ave., then winds past Evergreen Park before intersecting Hwy. 252.

- The route across Hwy. 252 is simple, but not immediately evident. After crossing Hwy. 252, take the sidewalk toward the bus stop. Look for an opening in the highway's sound wall that cuts through to the quiet, smooth bike trail along West River Rd.
- Turn left to ride north along West River Rd. for about 3.25 miles to the Hwy. 610 bridge. Just before crossing over 610, turn left away from West River Rd. to get on the freeway bridge and cross over the river. On the east side of the river, the trail forks. Take the right fork, which loops back under 610. This heads north (stay left at the trail junction) for over a mile through the park to return to the Coon Rapids Dam. A ride across the dam returns you to the ride start.

Point of Interest ➜ : There is an observation platform and informational plaque south of the East Visitor Center (mile 13.7). Located along the Mississippi, it offers an excellent view of the Coon Rapids Dam.

Extended Activities:

- Coon Rapids Dam Regional Park (ride start) has lots of great activities for nature lovers. Both sides of the river have staffed nature centers and offer miles of woodland hiking trails, great views of the Mississippi, wildlife viewing, fishing and geocaching, with GPS units available to borrow at the West Visitor Center or to rent at the East Visitor Center.
- Springbrook Nature Center, 100 85th Ave. NW, Fridley, 55432. Located just 3 miles southeast of the Coon Rapids Dam, this nature center features 127 acres, with an interpretive center, live animal displays, and dozens of educational programs.

Jon's Notes: This ride starts at the Coon Rapids Dam Regional Park Visitor Center. There are actually two visitor centers in the park—one on the east side of the dam run by Anoka County, and the other on the west side, run by Hennepin County. Both are fine facilities, but parking at the West Visitor Center is free, and that's where the map and directions show the ride beginning.

The first mile of this route, leaving the park and riding along the Rush Creek Trail, feels almost like wilderness. By contrast, the trails along Nobel and Xerxes are a mixture of blacktop and concrete, are crossed by many local streets and some driveways, and can feel a bit like sidewalks at times. At the same time, they are flat and open, offering good views, and there are no blind intersections or other surprises. While not the most picturesque segment of the route, this makes for a comfortable ride. Faster riders without young children, however, may prefer riding in the street along these sections.

When you turn off of Xerxes onto the trails through Palmer Lake Park, it feels like you have been teleported out of the city and into the wilderness. The flat, concrete-covered surroundings instantly give way to secluded woods, streams and wetlands. Don't be surprised if you end up sharing the trail with deer, turkeys or other wildlife.

After leaving Palmer Lake Park, the ride covers a few more miles on local trails through mostly residential areas before crossing Hwy. 610 to return to Coon Rapids Dam Regional Park. This final section of the trail offers beautiful views of the river and is a great place to watch for hawks.

Coon Rapids Dam Trail Environment

The "feel" of this route

YELLOW—urban areas or along busy streets

BLUE—suburban areas or neighborhoods

GREEN—parks, parkways and rural or natural settings

GPS Coordinates

- ⊛ Start/End (Coon Rapids Dam Regional Park): 45° 8' 25.59" N 93° 18' 53.10" W
- ◉ Rest Stop (West Palmer Lake Park): 45° 5' 2.70" N   93° 19' 25.17" W
- → Point of Interest (observation platform): 45° 8' 30.42" N 93° 18' 13.10" W

Follow meandering Rice Creek through a wooded valley in the heart of suburbia

Why Jon Recommends this Ride: Rice Creek West Regional Trail is a gem among metro area bikeways. Tucked away in the northern suburbs, it winds its way from Locke Park in Fridley to Long Lake Park in New Brighton. Much of the trail follows a wooded corridor along the twisting, winding banks of Rice Creek. This ride starts at Long Lake Park and loops around to pick up the Rice Creek Trail for the final 4 miles.

Tips: There is a large picnic shelter at the rest stop in Locke Park, but there's nowhere to get food nearby. Be sure to pack a snack if you want one for the rest stop.

Length: 11 miles, with an option of 8.2 miles

Location: New Brighton, Mounds View, Fridley

Terrain: Flat to gently rolling terrain with one very short (but very steep) hill near the end.

Considerations: At mile 8.5, there are two bike paths where the Rice Creek Trail crosses Central Ave. Only the trail on the east side of the street connects to our route. Be sure to cross Central Ave. first, then turn right to continue on the Rice Creek Trail.

Start Location ⊛: Long Lake Regional Park, 1500 Old Hwy. 8, New Brighton, 55112. Long Lake Regional Park covers 271 acres and includes recreational facilities and natural areas. It is a great place for a picnic for almost any size of group, and it's a great place to start a bike ride along the beautiful Rice Creek Trail. Amenities include parking, indoor restrooms, drinking fountains, a picnic shelter, a playground, and a swimming beach. Concessions are available in the main beach building, which is open Memorial Day through Labor Day.

Connecting Routes in this Book: None.

Route Options:

8.2 miles Shorten the route by 2.8 miles and skip the rest area by turning south on the bike trail along Central Ave. at mile 5.1. Rejoin the main route where the Rice Creek Trail crosses Central at 69th St.

The swimming beach also makes a great start location for a family ride.

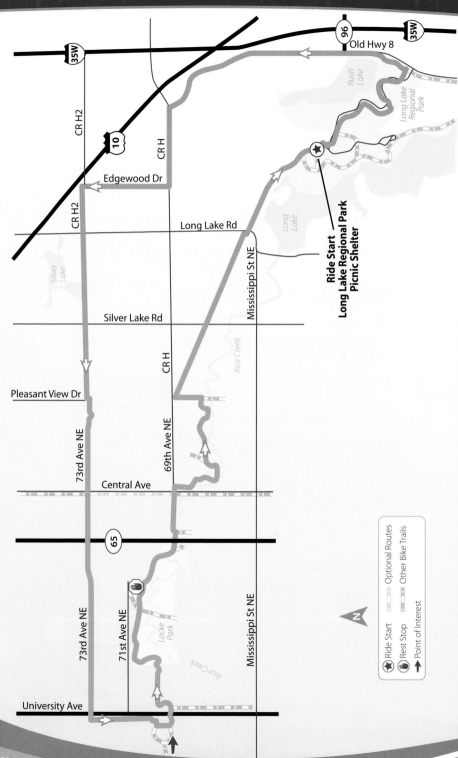

Step by Step Directions:

- Begin the ride by following the bike trail southeast toward the main entrance of Long Lake Park.

- From the park's main entrance turn left to follow the path along Old Hwy. 8. After a short distance, the path becomes a sidewalk but remains suitable for bicycles.

- Turn left on County Rd. H and follow it to Edgewood Dr.

- Turn right to cross County Rd. H and follow Edgewood Dr. to County Rd. H2. Edgewood does not offer a bike lane, but it is a low-traffic residential street suitable for nearly any rider.

- Cross County Rd. H2 at the crosswalk and turn left onto the adjacent bike trail. Follow the trail west along H2 for just under 3 miles to University Ave.

- The trail jogs to the left to cross County Rd. H2 at its intersection with Pleasant View Dr. (mile 4.6). Pleasant View Dr. is a small residential street and not an obvious place for a change in the trail. It is, however, the border between Mounds View and Fridley. Apparently, the city of Mounds View wanted the bike trail on the north side of the street, while the city of Fridley wanted it on the south side. Note that County Rd. H2 also changes to 73rd Ave. NE at this intersection.

- Cross University Ave., then turn left to head south along the bike path. After about half a mile, the path jogs across the frontage road and skirts the edge of Community Park. Turn left at the edge of the pond, then left again to exit the park and head back toward University Ave.

- After crossing University Ave., follow the left-hand branch of the trail, which curves north, then east before entering Locke Park. Our route follows the paved trail along the northern edge of the park, but adventurous riders may wish to explore the unpaved southern trail as well. Follow the trail another half a mile through the park to the rest stop at the picnic shelter.

Rest Stop ⊚: Locke Park picnic shelter (mile 7.8), 450 71st Ave. NE, Fridley, 55432. Locke Park is densely wooded and home to a winding stretch of Rice Creek. Amenities include a picnic shelter, restrooms, a drinking fountain and a playground.

- From the picnic shelter, follow the bike trail east through the wooded flood-plain of Rice Creek.

- The Rice Creek Trail passes through a tunnel under Hwy. 65, then crosses Central Ave. at street level. There are bike paths along both sides of the street.

Be sure to cross the street first, then turn right on the east side of Central to continue along the Rice Creek Trail.

- Around mile 9.5 the trail curves north, away from the creek, and empties out onto a small street. Follow the street for 50 yards, crossing the railroad tracks, then turn right to follow the bike trail along the rail corridor.
- The trail follows the tracks for 1.5 miles to the edge of Long Lake Park. This final section of the trail is flat and smooth. As it enters Long Lake Park, the trail crosses over Rice Creek one final time, then climbs a short hill before winding its way back to the picnic shelter.

Point of Interest ➔: Rice Creek West Regional Trail (miles 7.5–9.5) parallels Rice Creek, which twists and turns sharply through its undulating, wooded floodplain.

Extended Activities:

- Long Lake Regional Park (ride start): Nature buffs are sure to enjoy the natural areas in Long Lake Park, including cattail marshes, oak woods, the undeveloped shoreline of Rush Lake, and a 9-acre restored prairie. In addition to these beautiful natural areas, the park offers a number of other recreational opportunities. The swimming beach is open from Memorial Day through Labor Day. The beach building offers concessions, indoor restrooms, showers and changing rooms. There is a small picnic area next to the beach. The New Brighton History Center is a free museum located in the historic Bulwer Junction Train Depot, built in 1887. The museum collection focuses on railroad artifacts and includes a 1940s era caboose, a refurbished railroad work cart, baggage carts and a mail cart. Private tours are also available. A boat launch is located on the southern shore of Long Lake. It features a parking area for trailers, a concrete boat ramp, restrooms and a fishing pier.
- Carmike Wynnsong 15 Cinema (mile 3.5), 2430 Highway 10, Mounds View, 55112. This was one of the first theaters in the Twin Cities built with stadium seating. Today, the decor feels a bit dated, but the discount prices are just right for a family outing. There is a small bike rack next to the main entrance.

Jon's Notes: The bike trail networks of Fridley and New Brighton are not as developed as in other parts of the metro, but these two suburbs are home to one of the most beautiful trails in the Twin Cities, the Rice Creek West Regional Trail. I only discovered this gem recently; most of my rides through these northern suburbs cut across Rice Creek, rather than follow along it. And what a wonderful discovery it has been.

Rice Creek flows for 46 miles through the north metro, from its source at Clear Lake in Washington County to its junction with the Mississippi River in Fridley. The Rice Creek West Regional Trail follows the western portion of the creek. Although the creek flows through suburban Fridley and New Brighton, much of floodplain remains undeveloped, is heavily wooded, and offers some tranquil seclusion. A ribbon of green in the middle of suburban development, Rice Creek hosts a wide variety of migrating birds during the spring and fall, including eagles, herons, cormorants, warblers and even pelicans.

Rice Creek West Trail Environment

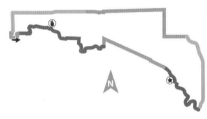

The "feel" of this route

YELLOW—urban areas or along busy streets

BLUE—suburban areas or neighborhoods

GREEN—parks, parkways and rural or natural settings

GPS Coordinates

⊛ Start/End (Long Lake Regional Park):
  45° 4' 52.61" N   93° 11'57.73" W

ⓘ Rest Stop (Locke Park): 45° 5' 45.86" N   93° 15' 1.84" W

➜ Point of Interest (Rice Creek West Regional Trail): 45° 5' 40.19" N   93° 15' 45.25" W

Follow the ribbon of green that connects the Mississippi River to Elm Creek Park

Why Jon Recommends this Ride: This is one of the longer rides in the book, but it is also one of the easiest to shorten. The main section of the ride is an out-and-back along the Rush Creek Trail, which stretches 7 miles from Coon Rapids Dam to Elm Creek Park. The wide, smooth trails avoid most major roads and most of the route is completely flat, making it a fine choice for single-speed bikes or riders towing trailers.

Tips: You can start your ride at the Coon Rapids Dam East Visitor Center and still park for free by parking on the street just outside the park entrance. It's a quick ride on your bike to the Visitor Center.

Since the main portion of this ride is out-and-back along the Rush Creek Trail, you can turn around at any point if you want a shorter ride.

Rush Creek Lollipop

Length: 18 miles, with longer and shorter options available

Location: Brooklyn Park, Maple Grove

Terrain: Rush Creek Trail is almost completely flat. The trails in Elm Creek park are rolling.

Considerations: There is an extensive trail network in Elm Creek Park, and it is easy to extend your ride—either on purpose or by accident! Staying right at each trail junction will keep you on the route, but it's a good idea to keep a close eye on the map, and watch for trail maps posted at most of the major trail junctions in the park.

Start Location ⭐: Coon Rapids Dam Regional Park Visitor Center West, Three Rivers Park District, 10360 West River Rd., Brooklyn Park, 55444. The East Visitor Center is run by Anoka County Parks, 9750 Egret Blvd., Coon Rapids, 55433. Amenities include free parking (the East Visitor Center has pay parking), restrooms, drinking fountains, a nature center, picnic facilities, and bike rentals for use in the park (at the East Visitor Center). The visitor centers also sell candy bars and soda.

Connecting Routes in this Book:

Elm Creek Park (page 146) shares a short segment at the midpoint of this ride.

Coon Rapids Dam (page 44) shares a starting point and a short segment at the beginning and end of this ride.

Route Options:

Shorter than 14 miles For a short ride, turn back at any point along the Rush Creek Trail.

14 miles For a 14-mile ride, skip the "lollipop" loop in Elm Creek Park.

18 miles-plus For a longer ride, extend the loop inside of Elm Creek Park (page 146) or add the small Coon Rapids Dam loop to turn the ride into a 22-mile dumbbell (page 44).

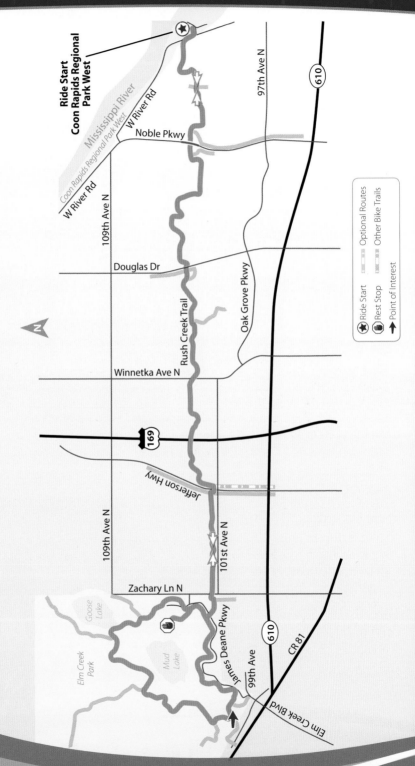

**Ride Start
Coon Rapids Regional
Park West**

Mississippi River

Coon Rapids Regional Park West

W River Rd

W River Rd

Noble Pkwy

109th Ave N

97th Ave N

610

Douglas Dr

Rush Creek Trail

Oak Grove Pkwy

Winnetka Ave N

169

Jefferson Hwy

109th Ave N

101st Ave N

Zachary Ln N

James Deane Pkwy

Elm Creek Park

Goose Lake

Mud Lake

99th Ave

610

CR 81

Elm Creek Blvd

N

⊛ Ride Start
✊ Rest Stop
↑ Point of Interest

▯ Optional Routes
▯ Other Bike Trails

Step by Step Directions:

- This route begins at the Coon Rapids Dam Visitor Center, on the west side of the river. You can also begin the ride from the East Visitor Center and start by riding across the dam. This is a scenic addition, though it adds a bit of distance and you may need to pay for parking on the Anoka County side of the park. Either way, as you leave the parking lot on the west side, you will cross over West River Rd. to pick up the Rush Creek Trail.

- The Rush Creek Trail then twists and winds west for 7 miles all the way to Elm Creek Park. The trail is almost completely flat. In fact, the largest "hill" on the trail is a wooden bridge where the trail crosses over Hwy. 169. The trail crosses a few local streets at grade, but goes over or under most larger roads.

- After crossing Zachary Ln., the trail enters Elm Creek Park and ends at a "T" junction with the park's trail system.

- Turn left at the "T," then stay right at each of the following trail junctions to complete the "lollipop" loop.

- Toward the end of the loop, another right turn will take you to the rest stop at the park's general recreation area.

Rest Stop (✋): Elm Creek Park General Recreation Area (mile 10.8), 12400 James Deane Pkwy., Maple Grove, 55369. The general recreation area at Elm Creek Park, located near the junction with the Rush Creek Trail, makes a great mid-ride stop. In the summer, there is a concessions stand at the swimming pond located at the north end of the parking lot. Amenities include picnic facilities, restrooms, drinking fountains, a playground, and a man-made swimming pond.

- Leaving the picnic area, the route continues south a short distance before turning left out of the park to pick up the Rush Creek Trail again. The ride returns to Coon Rapids Dam along the same route—which you will find just as beautiful, smooth and scenic as you did the first time on it.

- When you get back to the start, be sure to go take a look at the dam if you haven't already. The scene is always impressive, and in the summer, the cool mist kicked up by the rushing water is particularly refreshing at the end of a long ride.

Point of Interest ➔ : History buffs will enjoy the Pierre Bottineau House historic landmark in Elm Creek Park (mile 7.8).

Extended Activities:

- Coon Rapids Dam Regional Park (ride start). This park has lots of great activities for nature lovers. Both sides of the river have staffed nature centers and offer miles of woodland hiking trails, great views of the Mississippi, wildlife viewing, fishing and geocaching. There are GPS units available to borrow at the West Visitor Center and rent at the East Visitor Center.

- Elm Creek Park (rest stop). Elm Creek Park is a gem of Hennepin County's "Three Rivers" parks system, spreading across 4,900 acres and featuring a wide variety of amenities for recreation and ways to connect with nature. The general recreation area, which is the rest stop for this ride, has picnic shelters, volleyball courts, a swimming pond, and a large children's play area. The man-made swimming pond features filtered, chlorinated water and a sandy beach (there is a small user fee).

Jon's Notes: The Rush Creek Regional Trail is one of the most successful recreational trail projects in the Twin Cities. When the land was first acquired for the trail, the area was covered by farmland. Today, the farms are gone and the trail now winds through residential housing developments. Because land was acquired before the area was developed, the trail corridor is one of the widest in the metro area, making it feel more rural than it actually is. This broad ribbon of green connects Elm Creek Park—the largest park in the Twin Cities—to the Mississippi River.

Rush Creek Lollipop Trail Environment

The "feel" of this route

YELLOW—urban areas or along busy streets

BLUE—suburban areas or neighborhoods

GREEN—parks, parkways and rural or natural settings

GPS Coordinates

- ✪ Start/End (Coon Rapids Dam Regional Park): 45° 8' 25.59" N   93° 18' 53.10" W
- ◉ Rest Stop (Elm Creek Park): 45° 8' 28.42" N   93° 25' 27.03" W
- → Point of Interest (Pierre Bottineau House Historic Landmark): 45° 8' 6.75" N   93° 26' 34.17" W

A suburban ride that passes by one of the most picturesque lakes in the metro

Why Jon Recommends this Ride: This ride through Shoreview and Vadnais Heights passes by Snail Lake, Turtle Lake and Sucker Lake. These lake names are a great reminder to slow down, relax, and enjoy the beautiful trails and shorelines along this route.

Tips: There are two great places to stop for a picnic along this route. You may want to pack your favorite lunch when you head out on this ride.

The trail along Gramise Road sometimes floods in the spring. I have never found it to be impassable, but I did pedal through water about a foot deep one spring.

Length: 15 miles, with options of 8.5 miles, 9.5 miles and 12 miles

Location: Shoreview, Vadnais Heights

Terrain: Flat to gently rolling terrain with a few small hills.

Considerations: There are a couple of unmarked trail intersections at the beginning of the route, so keep a close eye on the map. But don't worry, the trails are fairly short and a wrong turn won't lead you far astray.

The lowest point in the trail, just south of Gramsie Rd. at mile 10.9, can be prone to flooding in the spring. I have always found a way through, but at times I have encountered deep puddles here.

There is no bike path along the southernmost part of the route, from the bridge over I-694 to Victoria St. The roads are mostly residential streets and all very low traffic. There are sidewalks too, which some riders may prefer.

Start Location ⍟: Snail Lake Park beach and picnic area, 4191 Snail Lake Blvd., Shoreview, 55126. The developed section of Snail Lake Park includes two parking areas, one for the picnic pavilion and one for the swimming beach, just down the hill. Additional amenities include indoor restrooms, a playground, and a beach house. A seasonal concessions stand is located at the beach building.

Connecting Routes in this Book: None.

Route Options:

8.5 miles For an 8.5-mile route, skip the northern loop around Turtle Lake by turning right onto the bike trail along Hwy. 96 at mile 1.5.

9.5 miles For a 9.5-mile route, skip the southern loop by turning right onto the bike path on Hwy. 96 at mile 8.0 and return to the start along the outbound route.

12 miles For a 12-mile route, turn north through the tunnel under Gramsie Rd. at mile 10.9 and follow the wooded trails back to the start.

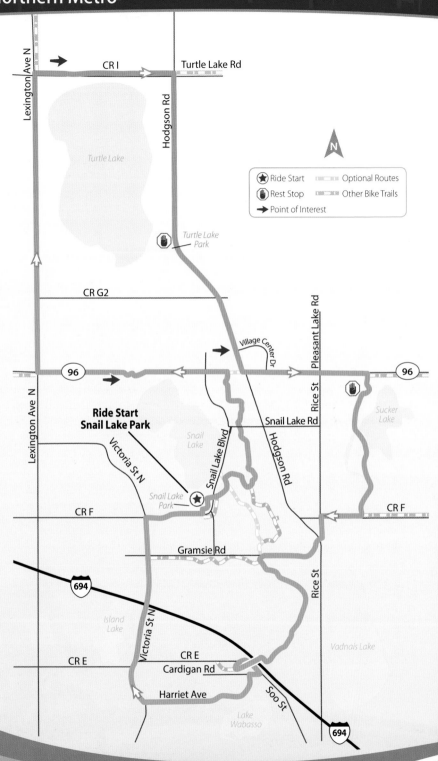

Step by Step Directions:

- This route begins on wooded trails just east of the Snail Lake recreation area. Though the scenery is lovely, be sure to keep an eye on the map. The route is easy to follow, but the trail intersections are not labeled.

- **Watch for this turn:** From the beach house parking lot, take the trail through the tunnel under Snail Lake Blvd. Follow the trail for 0.2 mile to a "T" intersection. Turn left at the "T," then take the next right.

- In 0.3 mile, at the three-way trail intersection, turn left and ride north for just under a half mile before passing through a tunnel under Snail Lake Rd. Then continue north to Hwy. 96, and turn left at Hwy. 96 and follow the adjacent trail to Lexington Ave.

- Turn right at the intersection with Lexington Ave., and follow it north to County Rd. I. Cross County Rd. I and turn right along the adjacent trail. The first few hundred yards of this trail are along a boardwalk. Continue along County Rd. I to Hodgson Rd.

- Turn south at Hodgson Rd. and follow the bike trail along the east side of the road to the rest stop at Turtle Lake Park.

Rest Stop 1(🖐): Turtle Lake Park (mile 7.0), 4979 Hodgson Road, Shoreview, 55126. Located on the shores of Turtle Lake, this park is well shaded by majestic oak trees. The park has been recently renovated and features many new and updated amenities, including a beach, picnic areas, indoor restrooms, a drinking fountain, and a playground.

- **Watch for this turn:** From Turtle Lake Park, continue south along Hodgson Rd. to Hwy. 96. Cross 96, then turn left to follow the bike trail east for just under one mile to the Sucker Lake picnic area. From Hwy. 96, the only way to access the Sucker Lake Picnic Area is via bike trail. Keep an eye out for the path on your right.

Rest Stop 2(🖐): Sucker Lake picnic area (mile 9.0), 4500 Rice Street, Vadnais Heights, 55126. For an alternative/additional rest stop, consider the beautiful picnic area at Sucker Lake, just south of County Rd. 96. Sucker Lake is one of the most picturesque lakes in the metro area. Its amenities include indoor restrooms, drinking fountains, picnic shelters, and a playground.

- From the Sucker Lake picnic area, follow the bike trail to the south end of the parking lot. Here, the trail joins with a St. Paul Water utility road. The road has a gate at each end to block car access, making it one of the widest and most picturesque sections of "trail" in the cities.

- Follow this "trail" south to the parking area off of County Rd. F, then turn right to follow County Rd. F west to Rice St. A left turn at Rice St. takes you two short blocks to the large intersection of Rice and Hodgson.

- Stay to the right as Rice St. curves toward Hodgson. Follow the bike trail straight across the intersection, where it continues along Gramsie Rd.

- Follow the trail along Gramsie Rd. as it curves and slopes gently downward. After about half a mile, the trails veers slightly away from Gramsie Rd. to intersect with a trail passing under the road. In the springtime, spring melt sometimes floods this low-lying trail junction.

- Turn left at the trail junction to circle around the wetland. As the trail rounds the marsh, it enters a narrow strip of woods, maintaining the natural feeling of the landscape right to the edge of the park. At the edge of the park, the trail emerges onto a bridge over I-694.

- Just after crossing the freeway, take the trail exit on the right to double back under the bridge and loop around to the intersection with Cardigan Rd.

- Turn right on Cardigan Rd. and follow it for one short block to Harriet Ave. Turn left on Harriet and follow it out to Victoria St. Note that there is no bike trail along Cardigan Rd. or Harriet Ave., which are both low-traffic residential streets.

- Cross Victoria and turn right to follow the adjacent trail north to County Rd. F. A right turn along County Rd. F returns you to the start at Snail Lake Park.

Points of Interest ➜ :

There is a small viewing area (mile 2.3) along Hwy. 96 that overlooks the undeveloped wetlands northwest of Snail Lake. The overlook is located across the street from the new Shoreview Community Center.

The route follows a boardwalk (mile 4.9) for a short distance along County Rd. I, passing over a small, undeveloped wetland.

If you would prefer a frozen treat instead of a lake view, you may want to stop at the Dairy Queen (mile 7.9) a mile down Hodgson Rd. from Turtle Lake Park. If DQ isn't to your taste, there are a number of other eateries located just across the street.

Extended Activities:

- Snail Lake Park (ride start): Snail Lake Park covers more than 450 acres, most of which is a nature preserve. The developed area of the park offers a swimming beach that has lifeguards on duty in summer, and a new beach house with changing rooms and concessions.

Jon's Notes: Whenever I ride through Shoreview or Vadnais Heights, I make sure my route includes the beautiful bike trails of Vadnais-Snail Lake Regional Park. These wide, smooth trails traverse wetlands, deciduous woods, and majestic stands of pines, while passing by some of the most picturesque lakes in the area.

Sucker Lake is, in my view, the most beautiful spot on the whole ride. The trail and picnic area are surrounded by stands of mature pines and the lake's undulating shoreline is almost completely undeveloped. Sucker Lake would look completely at home in the north woods and offers a lovely respite from the bustle of the cities.

Slow & Steady Trail Environment

The "feel" of this route

YELLOW—urban areas or along busy streets

BLUE—suburban areas or neighborhoods

GREEN—parks, parkways and rural or natural settings

GPS Coordinates

- ✱ Start/End (Snail Lake Park): 45° 4' 0.97" N 93° 7' 23.29" W
- ⊙ Rest Stop (Turtle Lake Park): 45° 5' 30.21" N 93° 7' 37.79" W
- ⊙ Rest Stop (Sucker Lake Park): 45° 4' 39.90" N 93° 5' 57.59" W
- → Point of Interest (Snail Lake Overlook): 45° 4' 44.20" N 93° 8' 7.77" W
- → Point of Interest (Boardwalk): 45° 6' 29.95" N 93° 8' 49.34" W
- → Point of Interest (Dairy Queen): 45° 4' 51.84" N 93° 7' 6.49" W

This long and varied ride ends on the most beautiful section of bike trail in the metro

Why Jon Recommends this Ride: This is one of the more challenging rides in the book. There are no facilities at the ride start, the route is the longest loop in the collection, and it involves a couple of tricky turns and a segment of street-riding along a county road. Even so, it also has a lot to offer, including what I consider to be the single most beautiful section of bike trail in the entire metro area, which comes at the very end of the ride.

Tips: If you prefer to have some facilities at the beginning or end of your ride, consider starting at the small commercial area near the intersection of Rice Creek Pkwy. and 85th Ave., located 1 mile north of County Rd. I. Here you will find a convenience store and a small assortment of restaurants.

Length: 18 miles, with an option of 4 miles

Location: Shoreview, Blaine, Lexington

Terrain: This is one of the flattest routes in the collection, with very few inclines and no real hills of any kind.

Considerations: Make a special note to jog east across Lexington Ave. at North Rd./101st Ave., just south of the I-35W overpass. The trail on the west side of Lexington disappears without warning half a mile farther along, with no easy way to cross to the east side.

This is a long ride with few amenities. Plan to be self-sufficient for most of this route, especially if you ride early or late in the season, when the boathouse at Lakeside Commons Park is closed.

Start Location ⊛: Rice Creek North Regional Trail parking area, Shoreview, 55126. The trailhead is located on the north side of County Rd. 1, just east of I-35W. This simple trailhead parking area has minimal facilities. There is a map of the nearby trails, but no drinking water or restrooms. A convenience store and a few restaurants are located just over a mile north at Rice Creek Pkwy. and 85th Ave.

Connecting Routes in this Book: None.

Route Options:

4 miles For a very short 4-mile route that still includes the beautiful trail near Rice Creek, turn right along 85th Ave. at mile 1.3 and follow it 1 mile east to rejoin the route at Lexington Ave. This short route can be extended into a 6-mile "mini-dumbbell" by riding the loop trail along Rice Creek just south of County Rd. 1. This 2.2-mile loop is not shown on the route map, but is very easy to follow.

125th Ave/CR 14

Lakeside Commons Park

Lakes Pkwy

Lexington Ave

CR 52

119th Ave

Radisson Rd

Lake Blvd

Sunrise Lake

N

109th Ave/CR 12

101st Ave

35W

North Rd

Radisson Rd

Lexington Ave

95th Ave

95th Ave/Lovell Rd

Jamestown St

93rd Ave

Service Rd

Woodland Rd

Lake Dr

85th Ave

85th Ave

Coral Sea St

35W

Lexington Ave

10

Rice Creek

Rice Creek Pkwy

Hamline Ave

Ride Start Rice Creek Trail Parking Lot

★ Ride Start   Optional Routes

✋ Rest Stop   Other Bike Trails

→ Point of Interest

CR 3/CR 1

Step by Step Directions:

- Turn right out of the trailhead parking area to follow County Rd. I west to Rice Creek Pkwy., which parallels I-35W. Turn right again to follow the trail along Rice Creek Pkwy. north to 85th Ave. Then turn left to follow the trail along the south side of 85th Ave.

- **Watch for this turn:** At the intersection with Coral Sea St., cross 85th and continue west for about 100 yards before turning right onto an unnamed bike trail.

- This municipal trail winds though a small patch of woods and wetlands before ending at 93rd Ave. Jog right (east) on 93rd to Jamestown St. and follow Jamestown north for one block until it dead-ends. At the end of the block, there is a cut-through to the trail along Radisson Rd. Turn right and then left to follow Radisson Rd. north and west.

- Follow Radisson Rd. for 3 miles to Lakes Pkwy. Turn right at Lakes Pkwy. and follow it 1 mile to the rest stop at Lakeside Commons Park.

Rest Stop ✋**:** Lakeside Commons Park (mile 8.9), 3020 Lake Pkwy., Blaine, 55449. Set on the shores of Sunrise Lake, Lakeside Commons is Blaine's newest park and recreation area. Amenities include indoor restrooms, drinking fountains, picnic pavilion, a playground, a swimming beach, a "splash pad" play area, and canoe and kayak rentals. On summer weekends, there is a concessions stand in the boathouse.

- From Lakeside Commons, ride east along Lakes Pkwy. to Lake Blvd. Turn left onto the trail along Lake Blvd. and follow it north to County Rd. 14.

- Turn right on County Rd. 14 and follow it to Lexington Ave. **Caution:** There is no trail along 14, but there is a wide, paved shoulder for all but the last 100 yards when the shoulder becomes a turn lane.

- Turn south onto the trail along Lexington Ave. and follow it for 3 miles.

- **Watch for this turn:** At North Rd. (101st Ave.), a half mile past the bridge over I-35W, cross Lexington to get on the trail on the east side of the street. Keep an eye out for this turn. The bike trail on the west side of Lexington ends abruptly a bit farther down, leaving cyclists with no good way to cross the busy street.

- Continue south along Lexington for another 2.3 miles. Shortly after crossing over 85th St., the trail loops around to follow Rice Creek under Lexington Ave. As the trail emerges from the underpass, follow along Lexington Ave. for another 100 yards before taking a right turn onto the Rice Creek North Trail.

- **Watch for these turns:** This final section of trail through the Rice Creek floodplain is the highlight of the ride. There are three junctions in this short section of trail. Stay left at the first two junctions, then stay right at the third. And enjoy the views. This ride saves the best for last.

Point of Interest ➜ : The last 200 yards of this route pass through what I call the Cathedral of Pines (mile 17.5), a breathtaking stand of mature pines.

Extended Activities:

- Lakeside Commons Park (mile 8.9), 3020 Lake Pkwy., Blaine, 55449. This newly renovated city park in Blaine is a great place to spend a summer afternoon with the family. There is a picnic pavilion, a large playground and a swimming beach. The boathouse features a concessions stand and offers canoe and kayak rentals for paddling around Sunrise Lake.

Jon's Notes: This ride begins at the Rice Creek North Trailhead in Shoreview and traces a large circle through Blaine. On the way back it skirts Circle Pines and the postage-stamp-sized township of Lexington. The crown jewel of the ride comes at the very end as the Rice Creek North Trail passes through a stand of mature pines that tower over the trail. The first time I saw this section of trail was on a ride with my wife. We had been chatting and laughing most of the ride, then fell silent, stopped pedaling and just coasted as we entered this cathedral of evergreens. When we got to the end, we looked at each other and, without a word, turned around to ride though the stretch of trail again. Instantly, this became our favorite stretch of bike trail in the whole metro area. I hope you find it as beautiful and awe-inspiring as we do.

Take the Blaine Trail Environment

The "feel" of this route

YELLOW—urban areas or along busy streets

BLUE—suburban areas or neighborhoods

GREEN—parks, parkways and rural or natural settings

GPS Coordinates

- Start/End (Rice Creek North Regional Trail parking area): 45° 6' 31.36" N   93° 10' 59.33" W
- Rest Stop (Lakeside Commons Park): 45° 11' 34.80" N 93° 11' 31.21" W
- Point of Interest ("Cathedral of Pines"): 45° 6' 38.69" N 93° 10' 51.89" W

Ride the train into downtown and bike back along the Grand Rounds of North Minneapolis

Why Jon Recommends this Ride: Who doesn't love a train ride? Minnesota's first commuter train is bicycle-friendly, and connects to the Cedar Lake Trail in Downtown Minneapolis and to the Mississippi River Regional Trail at the Fridley Station. You can park in Fridley, take the train into downtown, and then enjoy a lovely ride back along the parkways of North Minneapolis and the Mississippi River.

Tips: Get information about bringing your bike on the train here: http://metrotransit.org/bike-n-ride-on-northstar.aspx.

Length: 15 miles

Location: Minneapolis, Brooklyn Center and Fridley.

Terrain: The route has several long, gentle grades and a few short hills.

Considerations: The trail around Webber Park that passes under Lyndale and I-94 can appear confusing, but it is easy to navigate. You can't go wrong if you just follow the creek under the highway. Once you are past I-94, turn left to head north along the river.

If you time it well, you can ride your bike first, then take the train back to your start location.

Start Location ★: Northstar Commuter Rail, Fridley Station, 6151 E River Rd., Fridley, 55432. Note: A second parking lot is available on the east side of the station at 6050 Main St., Fridley, 55432. Amenities at the ride start include free parking and covered and enclosed waiting areas with on-demand heating systems. (Restrooms are available on the trains.)

Connecting Routes in this Book:

Trails to Light Rails (page 38) shares a segment and the short route shares the endpoint.

Cedar Lake Express (page 140) shares a short segment.

Coon Rapids Dam (page 44) comes within 1 mile of this route along West River Rd.

Route Options: You may prefer to start your outing in downtown Minneapolis, instead of in Fridley. Parking is much easier in Fridley, so consider riding your bike or taking the light rail (see Trails to Light Rails on page 38) into downtown.

• Since the train only runs a few times each day, it is usually best to ride the train first and return by bike. However, as long as you time it well, you can also ride first and take the train back to your start location. This route can also be ridden as an out-and-back, turning around at any point on the ride.

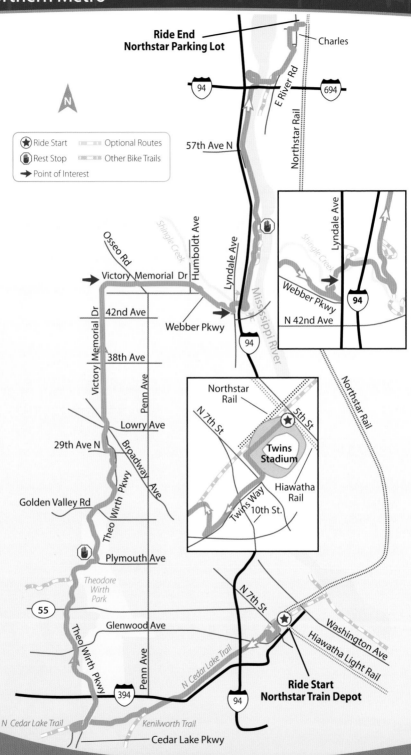

Ride End
Northstar Parking Lot

Charles

94

694

E River Rd

Northstar Rail

57th Ave N

★ Ride Start   Optional Routes
✋ Rest Stop   Other Bike Trails
➤ Point of Interest

Lyndale Ave

Shingle Creek

Lyndale Ave

Humboldt Ave

Osseo Rd

➤ Victory Memorial Dr

Shingle Creek

Webber Pkwy

94

N 42nd Ave

42nd Ave

Victory Memorial Dr

Webber Pkwy

38th Ave

Mississippi River

94

Penn Ave

Northstar Rail

Northstar Rail

Northstar Rail

N 7th St

5th St

Twins Stadium

Hiawatha Rail

Lowry Ave

29th Ave N

Broadway Ave

Twins Way

10th St.

Golden Valley Rd

Theo Wirth Pkwy

✋ Plymouth Ave

Theodore Wirth Park

N 7th St

55

Glenwood Ave

Theo Wirth Pkwy

Penn Ave

N Cedar Lake Trail

Washington Ave

Hiawatha Light Rail

★ **Ride Start**
Northstar Train Depot

394

94

N Cedar Lake Trail   Kenilworth Trail

Cedar Lake Pkwy

Step by Step Directions:

- The ride starts out westward along the Cedar Lake Trail, and follows the same BNSF Railway corridor as the Northstar. Though you can see the trail from the train, the trail entrance is on Twins Way, two blocks west of the Stadium. From the Northstar platform, take your bike up the elevator to the promenade and circle counter-clockwise around the Twins Stadium until you reach the intersection of N 7th St. and Twins Way. Turn right to cross 7th St. and follow the wide sidewalk along Twins Way for two blocks to the entrance to the Cedar Lake Trail. Turn right down the ramp, then turn left onto the trail.

- Follow the Cedar Lake Trail west for 2.4 miles, just past the north end of Cedar Lake and the Cedar Lake Pkwy. overpass.

- **Watch for this turn:** About 200 yards past the overpass, turn left to exit the Cedar Lake Trail, then turn immediately left again to follow the bike path back to Cedar Lake Pkwy. Curve left onto the trail along Cedar Lake Pkwy. and follow it north, crossing over the Cedar Lake Trail.

- The parkway changes names as it crosses over I-394 and enters Theodore Wirth Park, becoming Theodore Wirth Pkwy.

- Follow the parkway north for another 2 miles to the first rest stop—the Theodore Wirth Chalet.

Rest Stop 1✋**:** Theodore Wirth Park Chalet (mile 5.3), 1301 Theodore Wirth Parkway, Minneapolis, 55422. Modeled on a Swiss ski chalet, this icon of the park is worth stopping for, even if just to enjoy the architecture. Amenities at the rest stop include indoor restrooms, drinking fountains, a concessions stand, and indoor and outdoor seating.

- From the Chalet, continue north along the parkway. About 2 miles north of the Chalet, the parkway passes under a large overpass at Broadway Ave. and changes names again, becoming Victory Memorial Pkwy.

- Follow Victory Memorial Pkwy. north for another 1.5 miles, then follow it as it makes a right turn and continues east.

- Shortly after crossing Humboldt St., Victory Memorial Pkwy. ends at the edge of Webber Park. Jog across the street to continue east along the bike trail and circle around the park building.

- **Watch for these turns:** Just before the trail reaches Lyndale Ave., turn left to zigzag down toward Shingle Creek. Follow the trail along the creek as it crosses under Lyndale Ave. and I-94, then make a sharp left turn to head upriver through North Mississippi Regional Park, where you will find the second rest stop.

Rest Stop 2 (✋): North Mississippi Regional Park (mile 11.9), 5114 North Mississippi Dr., Minneapolis, 55430. This large park is a popular picnic spot for North Minneapolis residents. It has great facilities, including several picnic pavilions, a playground, and a wading pool. Amenities at the rest stop include drinking fountains and indoor restrooms.

• From North Mississippi Regional Park, continue north along the trail until it reaches the I-694 bridge over the river. After passing under the freeway, follow the trail across the cul-de-sac and up the slope as it loops around to follow the bridge across the river.

• After crossing over the river, the trail curves left to follow East River Rd. north. A few blocks farther—nearly in sight of the Fridley Station—the trail narrows and takes an odd detour around some apartment buildings. Stay with the trail; it swings back out to River Rd., right across from the train station.

Points of Interest ➔ : Victory Memorial Monument (mile 8.8). Victory

Memorial Pkwy. was built in the 1920s to commemorate Hennepin County residents who served in World War I. A beautiful new monument was built in 2011 at the bend in the parkway near Xerxes and 45th Ave. A block southeast of the new monument there is a statue of Abraham Lincoln, erected in 1930 by members of the Grand Army of the Republic to honor fellow soldiers who died in the Civil War.

Shingle Creek waterfall (mile 10.5). As the route exits Webber Park, it follows Shingle Creek under Lyndale Ave. and I-94. One attractive feature of this segment of the trail is an overlook of a tiny waterfall along the creek.

Extended Activities:

• Target Field (at the Northstar Depot), 326 7th St. N, Minneapolis, 55403. Enjoy a whole day outside by riding to a Twins game! Target Field has hundreds of bike parking spaces along the promenade. You can take the train to the game and ride your bike back, or ride to the game and take the train back.

• Eloise Butler Wildflower Garden and Bird Sanctuary (mile 4.1). First opened in 1907, the Eloise Butler Garden is the nation's first public wildflower garden. Created as a sanctuary for the area's native flora, the 150-acre garden hosts over 500 species of plants along its trails. The Martha Crone Visitors

Shelter offers natural history displays and maps of the garden. The garden's entrance is located just south of Glenwood Ave.

Jon's Notes: In the past few decades, "Rail Trail" projects have converted thousands of miles of unused rail lines into bicycle trails. More recently, the Metro has seen the arrival of commuter rail. The conjunction of these two movements is found next to the Twins Stadium in downtown Minneapolis, where the Cedar Lake Trail parallels the Northstar Rail.

This route covers the northwestern portion of the Minneapolis Grand Rounds—a series of bikeways that circle most of the city. The Grand Rounds was a favorite ride for my dad and me when I was a young teen. I always enjoyed the section of the ride along Victory Memorial Pkwy. The majestic tree-lined boulevard seemed exotic to me, like something out of another time. In a way, it is. The boulevard was constructed in the early 1920s as a memorial to the residents of Hennepin County who served in "The Great War." History buffs will enjoy the Lincoln statue and the WW I monument located at the bend in the parkway.

Trails to Rails Trail Environment

The "feel" of this route

YELLOW—urban areas or along busy streets

BLUE—suburban areas or neighborhoods

GREEN—parks, parkways and rural or natural settings

GPS Coordinates

⊛ Start (Twins Stadium): 44° 58' 57.90" N   93° 16' 39.70" W

⊛ Rest Stop (Theodore Wirth Park Chalet): 44° 59' 32.60" N 93° 19' 23.43" W

⊛ Rest Stop (North Mississippi Regional Park): 45° 2' 48.42" N 93° 16' 58.56" W

➜ Point of Interest (Victory Memorial Monument): 45° 2' 13.49" N 93° 19' 10.04" W

➜ Point of Interest (Waterfall): 45° 1' 58.68" N   93° 17' 19.28" W

End (Northstar Commuter Rail Fridley Station): 45° 4' 46.40" N 93° 16' 18.95" W

Ride as far as you like on one of the best "rails-to-trails" corridors in the state

Why Jon Recommends this Ride: The Gateway Trail is one of the premier bike trails in the Twin Cities. The 18-mile trail follows an old railroad right-of-way, so it avoids steep climbs, even in St. Paul's hilly East Side. It is wide and smooth and passes through stretches of wooded urban parkland, quiet suburbs, picturesque farms and pristine wetlands. Pick a starting point and ride as far as you'd like. You can't go wrong on the Gateway!

Tips: Although the trail has its western terminus at Cayuga Ave., the Gateway Trail Community Garden (trail mile 1.4) at Arlington Ave. is a nicer spot to park and to begin a ride.

While mainly used by cyclists, the Gateway is a multiuse trail. Please be courteous of other trail users, especially horseback riders who share the eastern portion of the trail corridor.

Length: 36 miles round-trip from start to finish, with options of 14.3 miles and 18.5 miles; by starting and turning back at different locations, you also can easily adjust the route

Location: St. Paul, Maplewood, North St. Paul, Oakdale, Pine Springs, Stillwater Township

Terrain: An old railroad corridor, the trail is either flat or follows gentle grades for its entire length. There are a few stretches that have a moderate slope, but there are no real hills.

Considerations: Few of the trailheads have access to drinking water, so be sure to bring enough for a long ride.

Start Location ★: Gateway Community Garden, 300 Arlington Ave. E, St. Paul, where the Gateway Trail crosses I-35E. Amenities include a parking lot, a drinking fountain, benches and a trail map.

Also, the 55th St. parking area at mile 8.6 is a great place to hop on the Gateway Trail. It is located on 55th St. east of Hadley Ave. at Hwy. 36 in Pine Springs, just before the trail crosses under I-694. Amenities include a parking lot, a drinking fountain, portable latrines, and a trail map.

Connecting Routes in this Book:

Phalen Inside & Out (page 98) shares a segment.

Route Options: As an out-and-back route with many trailheads, the Gateway Trail offers a wide range of options. Here are two that I particularly like.

14.3 miles For a nice ride through an urban and suburban greenway, start at the Gateway Trail Community Garden off Arlington Ave., then ride to the 55th St. Parking Area and back. The last couple miles slope downhill gently.

18.5 miles For a long ride through a more rural setting, start at the 55th St. Parking Area, ride to Pine Point Park (the ride turnaround) and back.

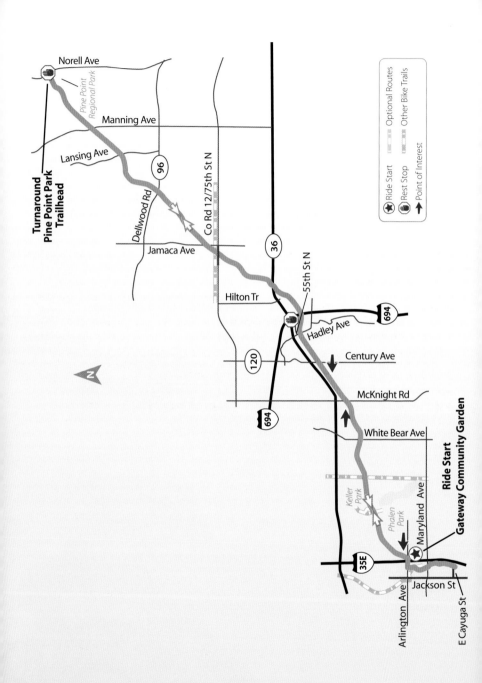

Norell Ave

Pine Point Regional Park

Manning Ave

Lansing Ave

96

Dellwood Rd

Co Rd 12/75th St N

Jamaca Ave

**Turnaround
Pine Point Park
Trailhead**

36

Hilton Tr

55th St N

694

Hadley Ave

Century Ave

120

McKnight Rd

694

White Bear Ave

Keller Park

Phalen Park

Maryland Ave

**Ride Start
Gateway Community Garden**

35E

Arlington Ave

Jackson St

E Cayuga St

★ Ride Start   Optional Routes
✋ Rest Stop   Other Bike Trails
↑ Point of Interest

N

Step by Step Directions:

- The Gateway Trail begins at Cayuga St., north of downtown St. Paul. For the first mile, the trail follows I-35E closely before crossing over the freeway and passing by the Gateway Community Garden, which I consider the best place to begin a ride on the Gateway.

- From the Community Garden, the trail crosses Arlington Ave., then begins a long, steady climb as it heads away from the center of the city. This segment of trail passes through a wooded corridor and has a very park-like feel, despite its urban setting. After about 1.75 miles the trail flattens out, then crosses over Phalen Creek and its adjacent bike path. This intersecting path connects the Gateway Trail to the amenities of Phalen Park (see page 98).

- Another 2 miles farther along, the trail crosses a high bridge over White Bear Ave., then passes by the campus of Maplewood City Hall.

- About a mile past City Hall, the trail passes by the North St. Paul Urban Ecology Center. You only get a glimpse of this restored wetland from the Gateway, but there is an informational placard next to the trail. A little farther on, the trail takes on a more suburban feel as it follows along Hwy. 36 for nearly 2 miles. Shortly after joining the Hwy. 36. corridor, the trail passes by "the Giant Snowman," one of the icons of North St. Paul.

- The trail branches away from Hwy. 36 as both approach I-694. There is a trailhead and parking lot just before the Gateway crosses under the freeway. This trailhead makes a good turnaround point for a ride on the suburban half of the trail, and an excellent starting point for a ride on the trail's rural half.

Rest Stop 1 👋**:** 55th St. Trailhead (mile 8.6), on 55th St. east of Hadley Ave. at Hwy. 36 in Pine Springs, 55128. This is one of the larger trailheads along the Gateway and the most popular. Amenities include free parking, portable latrines, a drinking fountain and a trail map.

- From the 55th St. Trailhead, the Gateway crosses under I-694, then Hwy. 36. Beyond Hwy. 36, the Gateway has a thoroughly rural feel to it. From this point on, there is a horseback trail parallel to the paved trail. For the first few miles, the trail passes through woods and wetlands, with an occasional glimpse of a large private home. Two miles past Hwy. 36, the Gateway passes under County Rd. 12. A short distance later, there is a small trailhead at Jamaca Ave.

- The landscape past Jamaca Ave. is more open, as the trail passes by a number of farms. The amenities are few and far between here, with a modest trailhead at Hwy. 96 and a pit stop at Lansing Ave. The rural scenery continues all the way to the end of the trail at Pine Point Park.

Rest Stop 2(🖐): Pine Point Park (mile 17.9), 11900 Norell Ave N, Stillwater, 55028. This rustic park marks the end of the Gateway. The park includes a small, modestly developed trailhead, right at the end of the trail. Amenities include indoor restrooms, drinking fountains, picnic tables, and benches. (A Washington County vehicle permit is required to park at Pine Point Park.)

Points of Interest ➔ : Gateway Trail Community Garden (mile 1.4) is a partnership between the Payne Phalen neighborhood and the DNR. Located on DNR land and maintained by local residents, the garden is the first of many "farms" along the Gateway Trail.

North St. Paul Urban Ecology Center (mile 5.9) is a recovered wetland. The site, which was once a sod farm, was restored to a pristine condition in the late 1990s to serve as a resource for environmental education. The site is open to the public and walking trails through the Center connect to the Gateway Trail.

The Giant Snowman (mile 6.9), located at Hwy. 36 and Margaret St., North St. Paul. This 44-foot-tall snowman sculpture, located just off the trail, has been an icon of North St. Paul since it was first constructed in 1974.

Extended Activities:

• Maplewood City Hall Campus (mile 5.0), 2100 White Bear Ave. N, Maplewood, 55109. The Maplewood Community Center is a great place for an active family to spend a day. Facilities include a swimming pool (for laps), a recreational pool, a gymnasium and a cardio center.

• Phalen and Keller Parks (mile 3.1), located on the east side of US-61, just north of Roselawn Ave., Maplewood, 55109. A spur trail off of the Gateway takes you into Keller Regional Park, which is connected to Phalen Regional Park by Keller Creek Park. Both of these parks make great starting locations for a ride along the Gateway, and both offer a wide range of outdoor recreation, including boat launches and fishing piers, golf courses, picnic grounds and numerous picnic shelters, an archery range (in Keller Park) and a swimming beach (Lake Phalen).

Jon's Notes: The Gateway Trail is one of the finest bikeways in the Twin Cites. Established in 1993, the trail stretches 18 miles from the heart of St. Paul to Pine Point Park just northwest of Stillwater. The "urban" half of the trail passes by a mixture of suburban development and parkland. The "rural" section of the trail shares the old railroad route with a horse trail as it rolls through marshes, woodlots and farms. The entire length of the trail is wide and smooth. This is an excellent choice for those with single-speed bikes or folks towing a trailer, and it is also great for in-line skating or rollerskiing.

When I was growing up, my family and I used to ride out to Stillwater every spring by following county roads near what is now the Gateway Trail. I fondly remember the sight of mist hovering over the marshes and the nearly constant chorus of red-winged blackbirds staking out their favorite cattail stalks.

Today, the Gateway Trail still passes through miles of wetlands and woods. On a recent springtime ride with friends, we were again greeted by misty marshes, a chorus of blackbirds, and something I never saw growing up—a small flock of sandhill cranes foraging in a field just past the Lansing Ave. pit stop. Even much of the "urban" sections of the trail have a wild feel to them. I often hear chorus frogs chirping from the ponds along the first 3 miles of the trail, and I have even encountered a pair of white-tailed deer just 50 feet from the trail's urban terminus at Cayuga St.!

Gateway Trail Environment

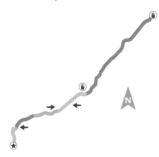

The "feel" of this route
YELLOW—urban areas or along busy streets
BLUE—suburban areas or neighborhoods
GREEN—parks, parkways and rural or natural settings

GPS Coordinates
- Start/End (Cayuga Street): 44° 58' 1.02" N 93° 5' 27.65" W
- Rest Stop: 45° 1' 35.54" N 92° 57' 47.76" W
- Turnaround/Rest Stop (Pine Point Park): 45° 7' 13.39" N 92° 50' 15.96" W
- → Point of Interest (Gateway Trail Community Garden): 44° 59' 2.50" N 93° 5' 16.43" W
- → Point of Interest (North St. Paul Urban Ecology Center): 45° 0' 23.98" N 93° 0' 27.85" W
- → Point of Interest (Giant Snowman): 45° 0' 55.12" N 92° 59' 30.68"

From a busy highway, through quiet neighborhoods, to a pristine wooded valley

Why Jon Recommends this Ride: After Woodbury, Cottage Grove has the best network of trails in Washington County. The trails serve much of the city, including the beautiful Cottage Grove Ravine Regional Park.

Tips: You can avoid the vehicle permit fee required for Washington County Parks by parking at the new Cottage Grove Public Safety/City Hall building located at 12800 Ravine Pkwy., just east of the intersection of 90th St. and Keats Ave.

There are no concessions at the rest stop at Highlands Park. Before you get there, you might want to pick up a snack at a convenience store at Point Douglas Rd. and 80th St.

There are two breaks in the Cottage Grove Trailway Corridor where the route follows a street for a short distance. Fortunately, the Trailway Corridor runs along a set of high-voltage electrical transmission lines. To stay on the route after the short stretch along Indian Blvd. and after crossing the Kingston Park parking lot, just follow the power lines.

Length: 11 miles, with an option of 9.2 miles

Location: Cottage Grove

Terrain: One long, steady grade, plus a few small hills.

Considerations: The route passes through a business district at mile 2, and another at mile 4. Use caution here when crossing streets and driveways.

The trail connections near Keats Ave., just south of 80th St., can be a bit confusing. You won't get lost, but you might end up taking a roundabout route. Check the map carefully—it won't lead you wrong.

Start Location ⭐: Cottage Grove Ravine Regional Park, 9940 Point Douglas Rd., Cottage Grove, 55016. This is a hilly, wooded park just off of Hwy. 61. The park is mostly wild and scenic and has one small developed area that serves as the starting point for our ride. Amenities at the ride start include parking (see Tips), restrooms, a drinking fountain, a picnic shelter, a fishing pier and a playground. A vehicle permit is required to park in the park.

Connecting Routes in this Book: None.

Route Options:

9.2 miles For a slightly shorter route, turn right onto the bike trail along 80th St. S at mile 4.3 and follow it to where it rejoins the main route at Joliet Ave., just before turning south onto Keats Ave.

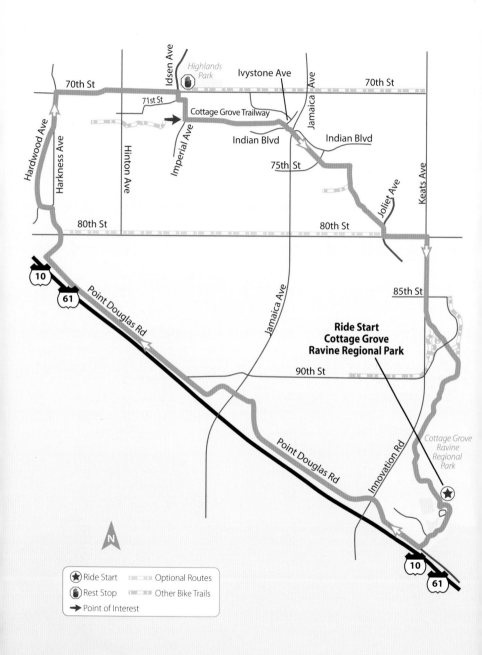

Step by Step Directions:

- This route begins and ends in Cottage Grove Ravine Regional Park. The majority of this park is undeveloped. Its steep gullies, unsuitable for farming, preserve the native oak forests that once covered the land near the confluence of the Mississippi and St. Croix Rivers.

- The ride leaves from the park's entrance along Point Douglas Rd., then heads northwest, paralleling US-61.

- At mile 4, Point Douglas Rd. makes a right-hand bend. The route follows, taking the sidewalk for a few blocks through the commercial district before crossing the street to pick up the bike trail again. The road changes names twice in about four blocks, but the route is straightforward and you end up riding north on the bike path on the east side of Hardwood Ave.

- At the intersection with 70th St., turn right and continue another mile to Highlands Park.

- The ride from Hardwood Ave. to Highlands Park is entirely uphill. It's not extremely steep, but it's a steady climb and you may be ready for a rest when you get to the park. Just remember that what goes up must come down.

Rest Stop 🖑**:** Highlands Park (mile 6.2), 6975 Idsen Ave. S, Cottage Grove, 55016. In addition to extensive ball fields, this city park features a small pond, which makes a great spot for a picnic. Amenities at the rest stop include indoor restrooms, a drinking fountain, a park building, and a playground.

- From Highlands Park, cross 70th St. and follow Idsen Ave. south into the residential neighborhood. Turn left at 71st St. and follow it to the intersection with the Cottage Grove Trailway Corridor.

- Follow the Trailway Corridor east, then southeast. There is a short jog along residential streets at Indian Blvd., and another through the parking lot at Kingston Park. Follow the power lines to stay on the Trailway Corridor.

- The Trailway ends at Joliet Ave. Turn right at Joliet, left at 80th St., then right at Keats Ave.

- **Watch for these turns:** Just past 85th St. the trail curves away from Keats Ave., then forks. Take the left fork here, which will bring you under a bridge. Stay right at the next trail junction to enter the ravine.

- As the trail slopes down into the trees, you will reap the dividends of the long climb up to Highland Park. For the last mile and a half, the trail descends gently through the thickly forested park, before emerging along the shores of Ravine Lake.

Point of Interest ➔ : Sections of the Cottage Grove Trailway Corridor (miles 6.5–7.2) are currently being planted with native prairie plants. Keep an eye out for trailside informational placards—and for birds and butterflies attracted to the indigenous wildflowers.

Extended Activities:

- Cottage Grove Ravine Regional Park (ride start): The majority of this 506-acre park is covered by undeveloped hills and heavily wooded ravines. The park's amenities include an extensive network of hiking trails and a small developed area with a picnic shelter, a large playground, and a fishing pier.

Jon's Notes: I first began riding through Cottage Grove in the early 1990s. My rides would often take me through Woodbury and across the now-decommissioned Rock Island Swing Bridge (see Concord by the Mississippi on page 128). These were typically long rides for me and I would usually stick to the county roads on the edges of town. Only in recent years have I discovered Cottage Grove's fine network of bike trails and the beautiful wooded slopes of Cottage Grove Ravine. This ride has an interesting character. The 11-mile loop takes you through the most heavily developed sections of Cottage Grove, along busy Highway 61, then loops up through residential neighborhoods and city parks, before easing you down into the pristine slopes of Ravine Park.

One of the first sights on this ride is a reminder of the ongoing suburban development: the entrance to the old Cottage View Drive-In is less than a mile outside Ravine Park. Up until the summer of 2012, Cottage Grove was home to one of only two drive-in movie theaters left in the Twin Cities. The Cottage View Drive-In first opened in August 1966, and lasted for 46 years before its final show in October 2012. The land has now been sold to a developer and the huge gravel parking lot of the venerable drive-in will be replaced with a big-box store that is scheduled to open in 2014.

The city's commercial district is past the old drive-in. Cottage Grove was first settled in the mid-1800s. Most of the prairie and oak savanna landscape was soon plowed and became home to some of the state's most productive wheat and dairy farms. A thriving community developed amid these farms, and this eventually developed into a bedroom community for St. Paul. The slopes of Cottage Grove Ravine, however, were too steep to plow and can be seen today much as they looked over 150 years ago. After circling through residential neighborhoods and suburban parks, the bike trail through the ravine carries you away from suburban development. The trail is just a little over a mile long, but as you descend into the park you feel like you are being transported into the deep wilderness. The trail finally emerges onto the nearly pristine shore of Ravine Lake, where you may want to spend the afternoon picnicking, fishing, or simply enjoying the solitude in the shadow of the city.

Groovin' the Grove Trail Environment

The "feel" of this route

YELLOW—urban areas or along busy streets

BLUE—suburban areas or neighborhoods

GREEN—parks, parkways and rural or natural settings

GPS Coordinates

- ★ Start/End (Cottage Grove Ravine Regional Park):
  44° 48' 21.76" N   92° 53' 58.46" W
- ⬤ Rest Stop (Highlands Park): 44° 50' 53.26" N   92° 56' 27.28" W
- → Point of Interest (Cottage Grove Trailway Corridor):
  44° 50' 43.14" N   92° 56' 22.91" W

Slip from the edge of suburbia into the forests and prairies of Lake Elmo Park Reserve

Why Jon Recommends this Ride: This ride takes you from the suburban parks of Woodbury through the countryside and into the pristine woods and savannas of Lake Elmo Park Reserve.

Tips: There are many great spots along the ride for a picnic but few places to stop to buy something to eat—so be sure to pack your favorite treats.

Lake Elmo Dumbbell

Length: 15 miles, with an option of 10 miles

Location: Woodbury, Lake Elmo

Terrain: A mixture of flat terrain and tiny hills. While a few of the rises are steep, they are also quite short.

Considerations: Keep an eye out for the turn onto the spur trail at mile 2.2. If the trail you are on passes next to the backyards of homes along a small lake, you have overshot it (but don't worry, it's only a tenth of a mile back).

If you go hiking or wander through tall grass on your stop in Lake Elmo Park Reserve, do a tick check afterward. This area is known to have deer ticks, which can carry Lyme disease.

Start Location ⭐: Edgewater Park, 3100 Edgewater Dr., Woodbury, 55125. A charming park that offers a beautiful view of the wooded shores of Colby Lake; amenities at the park include parking, picnic shelter, restrooms, a drinking fountain, a nice view of the lake, and a playground.

Connecting Routes in this Book:

Woodbury Wander (page 104) shares a segment.

Route Options: You can shorten the route by skipping the Lake Elmo Park loop, or by turning back at any point along the "out and back" section of the ride.

10 miles For a shorter 10-mile "lollipop" route, begin at Powers Lake Park.

• You can also do this ride starting at Lake Elmo Park Reserve. A Washington County vehicle permit is required.

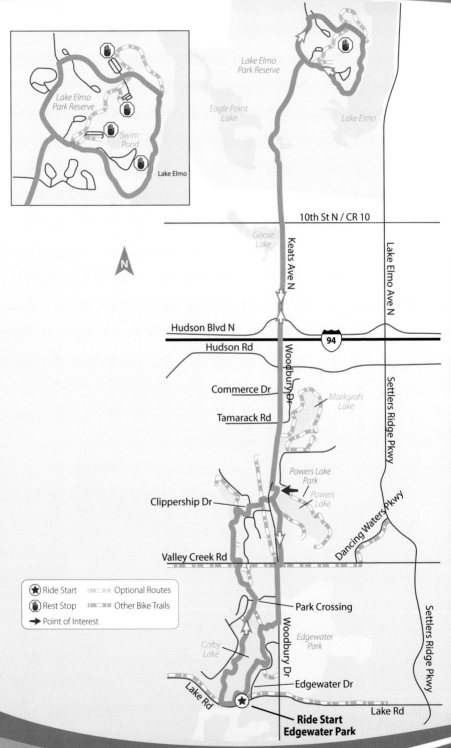

Lake Elmo Park Reserve

Swim Pond

Lake Elmo

N

Lake Elmo Park Reserve

Eagle Point Lake

Lake Elmo

10th St N / CR 10

Goose Lake

Keats Ave N

Lake Elmo Ave N

Hudson Blvd N

94

Hudson Rd

Woodbury Dr

Commerce Dr

Markgrafs Lake

Tamarack Rd

Settlers Ridge Pkwy

Powers Lake Park

Powers Lake

Clippership Dr

Dancing Waters Pkwy

Valley Creek Rd

★ Ride Start   Optional Routes
✋ Rest Stop   Other Bike Trails
➜ Point of Interest

Park Crossing

Woodbury Dr

Edgewater Park

Settlers Ridge Pkwy

Colby Lake

Edgewater Dr

Lake Rd

Lake Rd

★ **Ride Start
Edgewater Park**

Step by Step Directions:

- This ride begins in the small, picturesque Edgewater Park on the shores of Colby Lake in Woodbury. A bike path circles all the way around the lake, creating the southern loop of this "dumbbell" shaped route.

- To start, take the bike trail out of the southern end of the park, follow Lake Rd. for about 200 yards, then turn right onto the bike trail along the western shore of Colby Lake.

- At the northern end of the lake, keep left at the triangle trail junction to continue traveling north. You will cross a local street called Park Crossing then come to a trail junction. Follow the left branch of the trail, which takes you north to a tunnel under Valley Creek Rd.

- **Watch for this turn:** About a half mile after crossing under Valley Creek Rd., as you are passing a small lake on your left, turn right onto the spur trail. Keep an eye out for this turn. The spur trail will slope down toward a small pond before climbing back up into the surrounding neighborhood and ending at Clippership Dr.

- Turn left onto Clippership Dr. and follow it for a little over 100 yards before turning right onto another local bike trail.

- After one block, this local bike trail intersects a larger north-south bike trail in a small city park called Lakeview Knolls. Jog north (left) then immediately right to take the tunnel under Woodbury Dr. After crossing under Woodbury Dr., the trail emerges into Powers Lake Park.

- From Powers Lake Park, the route is a straight shot due north on the bike path along Woodbury Dr. The adjacent road is fairly busy until you reach I-94. Crossing over the freeway, the road changes its name to Keats Ave. and most of the suburban development falls away. As you continue north you are surrounded by the fields and pastures of rural Washington County the rest of the way to Lake Elmo Park Reserve.

Rest Stop 🤚**:** Lake Elmo Park Reserve, 1515 Keats Ave. N, Lake Elmo, 55042. Depending on your preferences, there are four places to take a break along the loop through Lake Elmo Park Reserve: the northern and southern picnic shelters, the swimming pond, and the main playground. Amenities at the rest stop include restrooms, a picnic shelter, playgrounds and drinking fountains. There is also a concessions stand at the swim pond that is open seasonally.

- The return trip follows the same bike trail south along Keats Ave. and Woodbury Dr. At Powers Lake, the route continues south along Woodbury Drive. It follows the east side of the street to Valley Creek Rd., then jogs across to the west side. If you want to pick up a treat for the end of the ride, you can stop at the small commercial area at the southeast corner of Woodbury Dr. and Valley Creek Rd. There you will find a convenience store, a drugstore and a couple of pizza shops.

- Half a mile south of Valley Creek Rd., the trail turns away from Woodbury Dr. and connects to the trail along the east side of Crosby Lake. Turn left when you reach the lake and follow the shoreline back to Edgewater Park.

Point of Interest ➔ :
Powers Lake Park (mile 2.8 and mile 13), 1400 Woodbury Dr., Woodbury, 55125. This park has restrooms, a drinking fountain and a small picnic shelter. This small park also makes a good ride start location for a shorter "lollipop" ride to Lake Elmo and back.

Extended Activities:
Lake Elmo Park Reserve (rest stop) covers over 2,100 acres in central Washington County and is an excellent destination for nature lovers and outdoor enthusiasts. Here is a sample of what the park has to offer:

- Hiking: The park features 20 miles of hiking trails that offer a variety of distances and difficulties.

- Orienteering: For more adventurous hikers, the park has three orienteering courses that range from beginner through advanced skill levels. Orienteering maps are available for purchase in the park office.

- Swimming: The man-made swim pond is a perfect blend of a swimming pool and a natural lake. Open daily from Memorial Day through Labor Day, it offers changing facilities, a sandy bottom, and has filtered, disinfected water.

- If you want to make a full day (or even a full weekend) of your outing, consider starting your ride in the park and taking advantage of some of the park's other amenities, such as the boat launch or fishing pier on Lake Elmo, the archery range, or campgrounds. A Washington County vehicle permit is required.

Jon's Notes:
Riding north along this route is a little bit like riding back in time. First, the suburban development of Woodbury gives way to the farms and fields of Lake Elmo Township. These in turn give way to natural woods, prairies and savannas of Lake Elmo Park Reserve. As you approach the park, the bustle of the city and the sound of the traffic fades and the quiet rhythms of the landscape take over.

While mostly left in a wild, natural state, the park reserve also has excellent recreational facilities. Either of the two large picnic shelters make a great rest stop. Both offer running water, electricity and nearby playgrounds. For a more active stop on your ride, check out the swimming pond or the large main play area.

The return trip offers a gentle return to daily life. The pristine landscape of the park reserve fades into the farms of Lake Elmo which, in turn, transition to the suburban development of Woodbury.

Lake Elmo Dumbbell Trail Environment

The "feel" of this route

YELLOW—urban areas or along busy streets

BLUE—suburban areas or neighborhoods

GREEN—parks, parkways and rural or natural settings

GPS Coordinates

⊛ Start/End (Edgewater Park): 44° 54' 9.80" N   92° 54' 35.44" W

◉ Rest Stop (Lake Elmo Park Reserve): 44° 59' 19.73" N   92° 53' 27.95" W

➜ Point of Interest (Powers Lake Park): 44° 55' 44.89" N   92° 54' 12.89" W

Why Jon Recommends this Ride:

The Phalen neighborhood on St. Paul's East Side is surrounded by some of the best bike trails in the metro, including the historic Gateway Trail and the Bruce Vento Trail. The Gateway was one of the first rails-to-trails projects in Minnesota, and established the precedent of using abandoned railways as non-motorized transportation corridors and recreational trails. The Bruce Vento Trail, which intersects the Gateway just northeast of Phalen, is a recent addition to the Twin Cities bikeways. These two major trails combine with the bike paths around Lake Phalen to make one excellent family bike ride. Phalen Park is one of the well-kept secrets of St. Paul's East Side. It has a swimming beach, fishing piers, expansive picnic grounds, a full 18-hole golf course and even a sailing school.

Tips:

There are several parking lots in Phalen Park. The map shows the ride from the beach house, but you can start next to the playground or the picnic grounds as well.

Length: 12 miles, with options of 3 miles, 7.7 miles, and 12 miles-plus

Location: St. Paul, Maplewood

Terrain: Mostly long, gentle grades with a few short climbs.

Considerations: The outer path around Lake Phalen is marked as a one-way path for bikes. However, on a nice summer day you can expect the whole trail to be filled with scooters, strollers, skates and bikes of every size and description going in every direction.

The Gateway Trail is closed south of the Gateway Community Garden trailhead at Arlington as part of the I-35E renovation project. This section of the trail is expected to re-open by the end of 2016. Until then, follow the Route Option for the I-35E Bypass.

Start Location ⭐: Phalen Regional Park, 1400 Phalen Dr., St. Paul, 55106. Amenities at ride start include parking (see Tips), drinking fountains, portable latrines, restrooms, playground, picnic facilities, and an 18-hole golf course. There is also a concessions stand in the golf course clubhouse.

Connecting Routes in this Book:

The Gateway Trail (page 80) shares a segment of trail.

Route Options:

3 miles For a very short ride, simply circle Lake Phalen.

7.7 miles For a shorter ride, cut across to the Lake Phalen bike trail at the intersection of Johnson and Wheelock Parkways, just north of Maryland Ave. at mile 7.4.

12 miles-plus To extend the route, ride out and back on the Gateway Trail or the Bruce Vento Trail from their intersection at mile 9.0.

I-35E Bypass: Turn left (east) on Arlington at mile 2.9 and follow it 1½ blocks to Arkwright St. Turn right (south) on Arkwright and follow it 1.3 miles south to Cayuga St. Turn left (southeast) on Cayuga St. and follow it 100 yards to return to the main route.

Step by Step Directions:

- Beginning at the swimming beach or the picnic pavilion, follow the bike trail along the west side of Lake Phalen up to the northwest corner of the lake.

- At the northern edge of Lake Phalen, turn away from the shore and follow the trail north along Keller Creek. After crossing under Parkway Dr. and the Gateway Trail, take a sharp right and follow the trail entrance up toward the overpass. At the top of the slope, turn right onto the Gateway Trail.

- The Gateway Trail is wider than the paths around Phalen. It is well maintained and well used, but rarely crowded. The Gateway descends gently, to the Gateway Trail Community Garden at Arlington Ave. Here, the Gateway leaves the Railroad corridor and follows Arlington over I-35E. Note: Due to construction on I-35E, the Gateway Trail is closed south of Arlington Ave. until late 2016. Until then, follow the I-35E Bypass outlined in the Route Options on page 97.

- After crossing I-35E, the trail turns left along L'Orient St. After about a block the trail turns right, away from the street. It continues south, passing under Maryland Ave, before reaching Cayuga St., just north of downtown St. Paul.

- At Cayuga St., turn left and follow the adjacent trail back under I-35E to Phalen Blvd.

- At Phalen Blvd., turn left onto Bruce Vento Trail. For history buffs, there are a few interesting historical markers along this section of the Bruce Vento Trail.

- The Bruce Vento Trail parallels Phalen Blvd. and climbs steadily to the rest stop at Eastside Heritage Park.

Rest Stop (🖐): Eastside Heritage Park (mile 5.6), 735 Phalen Blvd., St. Paul, 55130. This is a brand new park with a lovely picnic shelter. If you want a bite to eat, a grocery store and some fast food options are located on Arcade St. at the top of the hill. The park also has restrooms, a drinking fountain, and a picnic shelter.

- From the rest stop, continue east on the Bruce Vento Trail to Johnson Pkwy.

- Turn north along Johnson Pkwy., then continue along the Bruce Vento Trail as it passes by the south end of Lake Phalen. If you want to shorten the route, you can turn left off the Bruce Vento Trail here and follow the lakeshore back to the start.

- The Bruce Vento Trail continues north, away from the lake and major streets, to its junction with the Gateway Trail. Turn left onto the Gateway and follow it back to Keller Park.

- Retrace your route along Keller Creek and finish the ride by circling around the remainder of Lake Phalen.

Points of Interest ➔ : The Gateway Trail Community Garden (mile 3.0) has a parking area that is frequently used as a trailhead by cyclists and skaters on the Gateway.

Extended Activities:

- Phalen Regional Park (the ride start) offers a variety of year-round activities for families. There is a swimming area and a large sandy beach with a volleyball court. Farther up the shore from the swimming beach you will find a playground, a fishing pier, and spacious picnic grounds with covered tables and charcoal grills. The 18-hole Phalen Golf Course is open to the public and rents out equipment and carts.

Jon's Notes: This is my neighborhood ride. For over a decade, I have had the good fortune to live just a few blocks from Lake Phalen Park, right in the center of this route. Lake Phalen offers a picturesque backdrop for the start and finish of this ride.

I have spent countless hours biking, walking, rollerskiing and just sitting along the shores of Lake Phalen and nearby Round Lake. Ducks, geese, cormorants and herons are common sights around the lakes. In the spring and fall, I often see migrating loons and mergansers out on the water as well. Much of the shoreline is planted with native wildflowers, which attract a variety of song-birds and butterflies. Whether you are a nature lover, a history buff, a student of urban revitalization, or just a fan of great bike trails, you will find a lot to enjoy on this ride through my side of town.

Phalen Inside & Out Trail Environment

The "feel" of this route

YELLOW—urban areas or along busy streets

BLUE—suburban areas or neighborhoods

GREEN—parks, parkways and rural or natural settings

GPS Coordinates

⊛ Start/End (Phalen Regional Park): 44° 59' 2.45" N   93° 3' 18.85" W

⊛ Rest Stop (Eastside Heritage Park): 44° 57' 57.41" N   93° 4' 16.90" W

→ Point of Interest (Gateway Trail Community Garden):
44° 59' 2.50" N   93° 5' 16.43" W

Enjoy a variety of trails in one of the most bike-friendly cities in the metro

Why Jon Recommends this Ride: Nearly every major road in Woodbury is flanked by a bike path. This route just hits a few highlights of one of the most bike-friendly cities in the metro. Along the way, it passes along some beautiful wooded lakeshore and wetlands that are just off the beaten path.

Tips: The rest stop at Edgewater Park is a beautiful spot for a picnic, but there is nowhere very close to buy food, so be sure to pack whatever you would like to have along.

Length: 15 miles, with options of 12 miles and 15.5 miles

Location: Maplewood, Woodbury

Terrain: Rolling terrain with a few moderate hills.

Considerations: There are a number of intersecting trails in the wooded section of the ride just north of Valley Creek Rd. Keep a close eye on the map and directions here.

Start Location ⊛: Battle Creek Park, Waterworks parking area, 2401 Upper Afton Road, Maplewood, 55119. Battle Creek Park is the largest park in the Ramsey County park system and encompasses over 1,000 acres. Much of the park is wooded and is crossed by unpaved trails. Most of the modern facilities are concentrated near the Waterworks family aquatic center. Amenities include parking, indoor restrooms (at the pavilion), drinking fountains, picnic shelters and a playground. A concessions stand is available inside the Waterworks aquatic center for paying customers.

Connecting Routes in this Book:

Lake Elmo Dumbbell (page 92) starts at the rest area and shares a segment.

Route Options:

12 miles For a shorter, 12-mile ride, begin at the rest stop at Edgewater Park and cut out the loop around Battle Creek Park by following Weir Dr. to Valley Creek Rd., then going west to Century Ave.

15.5 miles For a simpler route that skips the wooded trails, turn away from Colby Lake at mile 7.6 and follow the trail along Woodbury Dr. north to Tamarack Rd. This option follows the return route for the Lake Elmo Dumbbell route (page 92), and adds about a half mile to the ride.

There are many other great options. Most major roads in Woodbury have bike trails alongside them—too many to include on our map. If you are feeling adventurous, try exploring some of them!

Step by Step Directions:

- From the Waterworks parking area in Battle Creek Park, follow the bike trail southeast to the intersection of Upper Afton Rd. and McKnight Rd.
- Turn south to cross Upper Afton Rd. and follow the trail along McKnight.
- Turn left at Lower Afton Rd. to continue circling around the park.
- At Century Ave., turn right to follow the bike trail south along the road. After about a half mile, Century Ave. curves to the left, then becomes Lake Rd. just before crossing over I-494.
- The trail along Lake Rd. switches sides of the street just after crossing over I-494, then it switches back a mile farther down at Woodland Dr. before settling in on the north side to take you the remaining 3 miles to the rest stop at Edgewater Park.

Rest Stop 🖐: Edgewater Park (mile 6.8), 3100 Edgewater Dr., Woodbury, 55125. This charming park offers a beautiful view of the wooded shores of Colby Lake. Amenities at the rest stop include a picnic shelter, indoor restrooms, a drinking fountain, and a playground.

- From Edgewater Park, ride north on the bike path along the east shore of Colby Lake.
- Keep right at the trail intersection just north of the lake to continue north across Park Crossing and into Colby Lake Park, which offers an alternate rest stop.

Alternate Rest Stop 🖐: Colby Lake Park (mile 8.1), 9715 Valley Creek Rd., Woodbury, 55125. Despite its name, Colby Lake Park is located well north of Colby Lake and does not offer any lake views. Its main feature is a large complex of athletic fields. Edgewater park is the prettier stop, but Colby Lake Park is closer to stores and take-out restaurants. There are several chain restaurants and a Holiday Station store located 0.5 mile east of the park (by bike trail) at the southeast corner of Woodbury Dr. and Valley Creek Rd. Other amenities at the rest stop include a picnic shelter, indoor restrooms and drinking fountains.

- From Colby Lake Park, take the bike trail through the tunnel under Valley Creek Rd. For the next mile and a half the route follows municipal bike trails through green space tucked between subdevelopments. Keep an eye on the map here. The route is not difficult, but there are no signs along the way.
- A half mile north of Valley Creek Rd., the trail passes by a small, unnamed lake. Follow the trail around the lake.

- **Watch for this turn**: At the north end of the lake, the trail makes a sharp turn to the left before dropping down a short but very steep incline. Take this with care.

- Just past this hairpin turn, the trail comes to a "T" intersection. Turn right at the "T" and follow the trail out to Interlachen Pkwy.

- Turn right onto the trail along Interlachen Pkwy. and follow it north to Tamarack Dr.

- Turn left onto the trail along Tamarack Dr. and follow it for a little over 2 miles, past the large commercial developments of Tamarack Village and across I-494 to Weir Rd.

- Turn left at Weir Rd. and follow the bike trail south to Upper Afton Rd.

- A right turn on Upper Afton Rd. takes you back to the entrance to the Waterworks parking lot.

Point of Interest ➜ :
Marsh Creek Heritage House (mile 5.0) is a historic house and a memorial garden. The house is open to visitors from 1 p.m. to 4 p.m. on the second and fourth Sundays in June through September.

Extended Activities:

- Battle Creek Waterworks Family Aquatic Center (ride start): This water park has something for everyone in the family and is a great place to cool off after your ride. Highlights include a giant lily pad walk, a twisting three-story waterslide, and shallow pools for young children. There is also a sunbathing deck and a sand-filled play area.

Jon's Notes:
Woodbury has always been a great place to ride a bike. In the early 1990s, when Woodbury was still mostly farmland, my cycling club would ride out along Valley Creek Rd., dutifully stopping for the single stop sign on the way. I remember the first day we encountered a newly installed traffic light, and over the years we watched as the corn fields gave way to suburban development. I feared that the area would be a loss for cycling, but I was mistaken. The city planners put real care into how the area developed and Woodbury now boasts the best network of bike trails in the east metro, with wide asphalt paths flanking most of the major roadways, and winding through many of the tranquil neighborhoods.

The parks in Woodbury are also first rate. Edgewater Park, which is one of the rest stop options for this ride, is a beautiful little city park on the south shore of Colby Lake. My last visit to the park was together with my mom on our tandem bike. We lingered for a long time at the picnic shelter, snacking on trail mix and sandwiches as we watched ducks dabbling in the shallows as two preschool-aged cyclists tossed them bread crumbs. Though most of the corn fields are gone, I still find Woodbury a pretty peaceful place for a bike ride.

Woodbury Wander Trail Environment

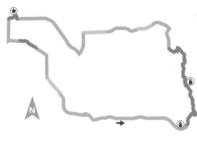

The "feel" of this route

YELLOW—urban areas or along busy streets

BLUE—suburban areas or neighborhoods

GREEN—parks, parkways and rural or natural settings

GPS Coordinates

⊛ Start/End (Battle Creek Park): 44° 56' 36.30" N 93° 0' 4.43" W

⧫ Rest Stop (Edgewater Park): 44° 54' 9.80" N 92° 54' 35.44" W

⧫ Alternate Rest Stop (Colby Lake Park): 44° 55' 4.78" N 92° 54' 32.69" W

→ Point of Interest (Marsh Creek Heritage House): 44° 54' 17.12" N 92° 56' 35.74" W

Three easy-to-follow loops on smooth trails, with a side trip to the Minnesota Zoo

Why Jon Recommends this Ride:
Eagan and Apple Valley each have an excellent network of bike trails along their major streets. This ride makes three loops along some of these outstanding bikeways. The route also swings past the Minnesota Zoo, which is a great destination for a family bike ride.

Tips:
Remember to bring bike locks if you plan to stop at the Zoo.

Length: 15 miles, with options of 9.8 miles, 10.2 miles, 13.2 miles and 16 miles

Location: Apple Valley, Eagan

Terrain: Rolling terrain with many short hills. This is one of the hillier routes in the collection and can be a challenging ride for bike trailers or those with single-speed bikes.

Considerations: This is a fairly hilly ride.

Start Location ⊛: Johnny Cake Ridge Park East, 5800 140th St. W, Apple Valley, 55124. Johnny Cake Ridge Park is a large complex that includes over 150 acres of athletic fields and also hosts the Apple Valley Teen Center and Family Aquatic Center. The ride begins from the parking lot for the eastern portion of the park. If you prefer, however, you can also park in the western part of the park, near the Teen Center and Aquatic Center. Amenities at the ride start include a picnic shelter (near the center of the softball complex), portable latrines, and indoor restrooms (that have limited hours).

Connecting Routes in this Book:

Highline Highlights (page 122) crosses the northern loop of this route at two points.

Bet the Farm (page 116) begins 2 miles south and connects to this route via the bike trails along Pilot Knob Rd. and Galaxie Ave.

Route Options: Shorten the route by cutting out any one of the three loops:

9.8 miles To shorten the route by 5.2 miles, cut out the loop around the Zoo by continuing straight south on Pilot Knob Rd. at mile 6.9.

10.2 miles To shorten the ride by 4.8 miles, skip the northern loop by turning left on Cliff Rd. at mile 3.1.

13.2 miles Cutting out the final loop and returning along Johnny Cake Ridge Rd. at mile 9.6 shortens the ride by 1.8 miles.

16 miles Adding a trip to the Zoo lengthens the route by about 1 mile.

Ride Start
* Ride Start
* Rest Stop
→ Point of Interest

Optional Routes
Other Bike Trails

N

Blackhawk Rd

35E

Deerwood Dr

Pilot Knob Rd

CR 30

Diffley Rd

CR 31

Johnny Cake Ridge Rd

Thomas Lake Park

Thomas Lake

Blackhawk Rd

Cliff Rd

Cliff Rd

Galaxie Ave

35E

Pilot Knob Rd

77

127th St W

Galaxie Ave

Diamond Path

Farquar Lake

McAndrews Rd / 125th St W

Johnny Cake Ridge Rd

Long Lake

Farquar Park

Cedar Rd

Pilot Knob Rd

**Ride Start
Johnny Cake Ridge
Park East**

140th St W

140th St W

Johnny Cake Ridge Park East

Step by Step Directions:

- From Johnny Cake Ridge Park East, begin by riding north along Johnny Cake Ridge Rd. to Deerwood Dr.
- Turn right to follow Deerwood east to Pilot Knob Rd.
- Turn right again to follow Pilot Knob Rd. south to the rest stop at Thomas Lake Park.

Rest Stop (✋): Thomas Lake Park (mile 6.6), 4425 Pilot Knob Rd., Eagan, 55122. Thomas Lake is a shallow, picturesque lake located where Pilot Knob Rd. intersects the Highline Trail (see Highline Highlights, page 122). It is a beautiful spot for a picnic. Amenities at the rest stop include a picnic shelter, restrooms, a drinking fountain, and a playground.

- From the park, continue south along Pilot Knob Rd. to Cliff Rd.
- Turn right along Cliff Rd. to follow it west to Galaxie Ave.
- Turn left on Galaxie Ave. to head south. After a little over a mile, the bike trail jogs right, across Galaxie Ave. Continue south along the trail for another mile to McAndrews Rd.
- Turn left at McAndrews Rd. The entrance to the Zoo is located on McAndrews Rd. at mile 11.5. There are bike trails on both sides of the street, and you can follow either one, but you will want to stay on the north side of McAndrews if you plan to stop at the Zoo.
- From the Zoo it is just 3.5 miles back to the start. To get there, take McAndrews east again, jogging to the trail on the south side of the road where it crosses Johnny Cake Ridge Rd.
- Turn right at Pilot Knob Rd. and follow it south to 140th St.
- A right turn along 140th St. brings you back to Johnny Cake Ridge Park

Point of Interest ➜ : Farquar Park (mile 13.6) is a small lakeside city park a bit over a mile from the end of the ride. It is a nice spot to stop if you need a quick break before the final mile. There is also a restroom, which is open seasonally, near the playground in the eastern part of the park.

Extended Activities:

- Minnesota Zoo (mile 11.5).13000 Zoo Blvd., Apple Valley, 55124. For over 30 years, the Minnesota Zoo has been helping people make connections with animals and the natural world. An innovator and leader in conservation and education since its inception, the Zoo is one of the best family destinations in the metro area. The zoo features two indoor trails and two outdoor trails of animal exhibits, a monorail, a large aquarium, and numerous daily demonstration and interpretive programs. Two exhibits—Monkey Island on the Tropical Trail and the beaver exhibit on the Minnesota Trail are among my perennial favorites.

- Apple Valley Family Aquatic Center (ride start). The family aquatic center is an outdoor waterpark with something for everyone. The facility includes wading pools, waterslides, diving boards, lanes for swimming laps, and more. It's a great way to cool off on a hot day, and it's located right in the Johnny Cake Ridge Park complex, across the street from the ride start.

Jon's Notes: My parents brought me to the "New Zoo" in Apple Valley when it first opened in 1978, and I fell in love with it. By the early 1980s my dad and I were riding our bikes to the Zoo from our home in Minneapolis, and to a 12-year-old the street names—Johnny Cake Ridge Road and Pilot Knob Road—were nearly as exotic as the animals. And these peculiarly named roads boasted some of the best bike trails I had ever seen. The bike ride was as much fun as the visit to the Zoo.

The Minnesota Zoo has grown a great deal since then, and I don't remember the last time I heard anyone but me call it the "New Zoo." But it is still a wonderful destination for a family, and the bike trails around the zoo are still first-rate.

This ride traces three loops through Eagan and Apple Valley, forming a kind of double figure eight. The entire ride takes place on wide bike trails that parallel prominent streets. Nearly every major street in this area has a trail alongside, so this is an easy route to modify if you choose.

Around the Zoo Trail Environment

The "feel" of this route

YELLOW—urban areas or along busy streets

BLUE—suburban areas or neighborhoods

GREEN—parks, parkways and rural or natural settings

GPS Coordinates

⊛ Start/End (Johnny Cake Park East): 44° 44' 44.58" N   93° 11' 3.71" W

◉ Rest Stop (Thomas Lake Park): 44° 47' 43.51" N   93° 10' 2.09" W

→ Point of Interest: (Farquar Park): 44° 45' 26.03" N   93° 10' 10.99" W

The simplest route in the book gives you a taste of rural Minnesota

Why Jon Recommends this Ride: This is an easy-to-follow route along wide bike trails on the edge of suburbia. This is one of the simplest routes in the collection—but not the easiest. The rolling terrain provides a bit of a workout, and the open landscape can provide a challenge if conditions are windy.

Tips: The section of Rambling River Park that we use as a rest stop on this ride is called "Northview Park" on Google Maps.

Length: 16 miles

Location: Lakeville, Farmington

Terrain: Rolling terrain with long, steady grades and a few hills.

Considerations: The terrain along this ride is rolling, not flat. While there are few substantial hills, on this route you are usually either going up or down a slight grade.

On these country roads, there is little to block the wind, which can make this a challenging ride in a strong breeze.

Start Location ⍟: Valley Lake Park, 16050 Garrett Path, Lakeville, 55044. Located next to a convenience store, and surrounding a small lake, this park makes a great spot to begin a ride with the family. Amenities at the ride start include parking, indoor restrooms, a picnic shelter, playground, a swimming beach, and a fishing pier. For food, there is a convenience store located just west of the park.

Connecting Routes in this Book: None. However, Around the Zoo (page 110) begins 2 miles north and connects to this route via the bike trails along Pilot Knob Rd. and Galaxie Ave.

Route Options: You can also begin this ride at Rambling River Park in Farmington. This can be an especially nice option if you enjoy trout fishing.

Valley Lake Park

**Ride Start
Valley Lake Park**

160th St

170th St

190th St

190th St

195th St

200th St

208th S

212th St

Lakeville Blvd

CR 50

Cedar Ave

Flagstaff Ave

Dodd Blvd

Pilot Knob Rd

Akin Rd

Flagstaff Ave

Rambling River Park

N

★ Ride Start   Optional Routes
⬤ Rest Stop   Other Bike Trails
➜ Point of Interest

Step by Step Directions:

- The route is very simple. From Valley Lake Park, ride west to Cedar Ave. Cross Cedar and follow the bike trail on the west side of the street south. Follow this trail all the way to County Rd. 50, which is also called Lakeville Blvd.
- Turn left to follow County Rd. 50 east to the rest stop at Rambling River Park.

Rest Stop⠀: Rambling River Park (mile 8.8), 99 Pine St., Farmington, 55024. This park on the edge of downtown Farmington surrounds the wooded shores of the Vermillion River—considered one of the best trout steams in the metro area. Amenities at the rest stop include indoor restrooms, drinking fountains, a picnic shelter, and a playground. A convenience store and a sandwich shop are located 3 blocks east of the park on CR 50/212th St.

- From the park, backtrack slightly along County Rd. 50 to pick up the bike trail along Akin Rd. Note that you will need to turn right onto the bike trail at the baseball diamond, a bit before you get to Akin Rd.
- Follow the trail along Akin Rd. north and west to Pilot Knob Rd.
- Cross Pilot Knob and turn right to take the trail on the west side of the road up to 160th St.
- At 160th St., in the shadow of an Apple Valley water tower, turn left to follow 160th back to Valley Lake Park.

Extended Activities:

- There are opportunities to fish at both the ride start and the rest stop. The Minnesota DNR stocks Valley Lake with bluegills, crappies, bass and northerns. There is a small fishing pier located near the northwest corner of the lake. If the fish aren't biting there, try walking around to the far side of the lake and fishing from the shore. The Vermillion River, which flows through Rambling River Park, is considered one of the finest trout streams in the metro area. Even if you just plan to catch-and-release, make sure you have a current Minnesota Fishing License with a valid Trout Stamp.

Jon's Notes: For many years, Dakota County has been a great place to bike, and it continues to get better. I have often headed out onto the county roads between Lakeville and Farmington when I wanted a long, relaxing ride away from traffic. Over the years, I have watched the network of bike trails in this area steadily improve. This ride makes a loop along some of these excellent trails.

On this ride, you will find yourself at the intersection between suburban development and small-town farmland. When I first started riding the roads in this area, it was clear that I was in the country—about as likely to be passed by a tractor as by a minvan. Now the beginning of the ride in Valley Lake Park is clearly suburban, and the route passes through a mixture of fields and subdivisions. Farmington, while definitely on the edge of the encroaching suburbia, still has a small-town feel to it and you might enjoy a detour into town at the midway point.

Bet the Farm Trail Environment

The "feel" of this route

YELLOW—urban areas or along busy streets

BLUE—suburban areas or neighborhoods

GREEN—parks, parkways and rural or natural settings

GPS Coordinates

⬟ Start/End (Valley Lake Park): 44° 43' 0.06" N   93° 12' 35.51" W

⬤ Rest Stop (Rambling River Park): 44° 38' 30.12" N   93° 9' 14.17" W

Explore some of the great parks and trails of the southern metro

Why Jon Recommends this Ride: The city of Eagan has been rated three times as one of the "20 Best Places to Live" in the U.S. by *Money* magazine. One reason, no doubt, is its excellent network of bicycle trails! Take a ride along some of the best bike paths in Eagan, highlighted by the picturesque Highline Trail.

Tips: The bike path along Blackhawk Rd. from mile 1.6 to mile 4.1 is crossed by a number of driveways and residential streets. More-athletic riders may prefer riding in the street.

Length: 14 miles

Location: Eagan

Terrain: This route has many short hills, especially along Highline Trail itself. Though short, many of the hills are steep.

Considerations: The turn from Blackhawk Rd. onto the Highline Trail is a bit tricky. Follow the map and directions carefully.

Highline Trail has many short, steep hills and includes some sharp downhill turns. Use caution.

Start Location ⭐: Eagan Community Center and Central Park, 1501, Central Pkwy., Eagan, 55121. The central feature of Eagan's Central Park is the expansive community center, which features parking, a fitness center, three gymnasiums, a space-themed indoor playground, and an information booth. Restrooms and drinking fountains are available. The park also has outdoor playgrounds, recreational fields, wooded walking trails, a picnic pavilion and a small gazebo that overlooks a large pond. If you're looking for a bite to eat, there are vending machines and a concessions stand in the community center. Note that the concessions stand has limited hours. There are also a wide variety of restaurants located in and around the Eagan Promenade, just a few blocks from Central Park.

Connecting Routes in this Book:

Around the Zoo (page 110) crosses this route in two places.

Scaling the Heights (page 134) passes 2 miles north of this route and is connected by the bike trail along Pilot Knob Rd.

Route Options:

If you want to finish the ride along the scenic but hilly Highline Trail, you can begin and end at the rest stop at Trapp Farm Park.

To avoid the short, steep hills on the Highline Trail, continue following Blackhawk Rd. (mile 4.1) to Cliff Rd. Turn left, following the bike trail along Cliff Rd. east to Lexington Ave., then turn left again. Follow Lexington north to Wilderness Run Rd. to rejoin the Highline Trail just before the rest stop.

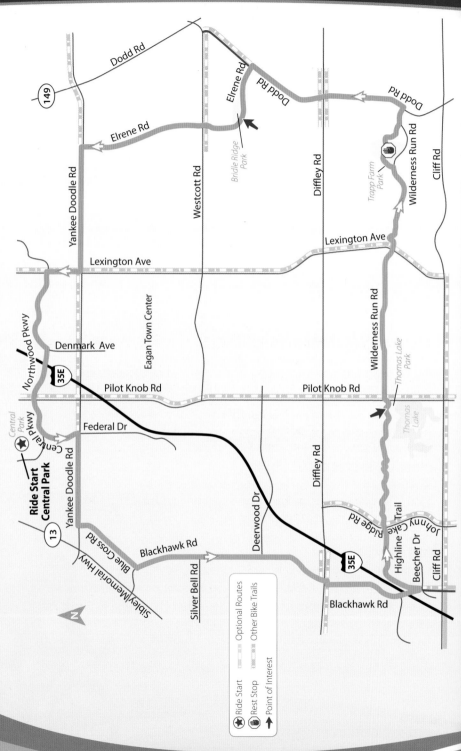

149

Dodd Rd

Elrene Rd

Dodd Rd

Elrene Rd

Bridle Ridge Park

Dodd Rd

Wilderness Run Rd

Cliff Rd

Westcott Rd

Diffley Rd

Trapp Farm Park

Yankee Doodle Rd

Lexington Ave

Lexington Ave

Eagan Town Center

Wilderness Run Rd

Thomas Lake Park

Denmark Ave

Northwood Pkwy

35E

Pilot Knob Rd

Pilot Knob Rd

Thomas Lake

Central Park Pkwy

Federal Dr

Ride Start
Central Park

Yankee Doodle Rd

Diffley Rd

Highline Trail

Johnny Cake Ridge Rd

Beecher Dr

Cliff Rd

13

Blackhawk Rd

Deerwood Dr

35E

Blue Cross Rd

Silver Bell Rd

Sibley Memorial Hwy

Blackhawk Rd

N

Ride Start
Rest Stop
Point of Interest

Optional Routes
Other Bike Trails

Step by Step Directions:

- From the Eagan Community Center, ride south beside Central Pkwy. to Yankee Doodle Rd. Turn right onto the path along Yankee Doodle Rd. and follow it to Blue Cross Rd.

- Turn left to cross Yankee Doodle Rd. and follow the trail along Blue Cross Rd. past the headquarters of the health insurance giant to Blackhawk Rd.

- Turn left onto the bike path along Blackhawk Rd. This trail passes through some of the older residential neighborhoods of this relatively young community. The bike path along Blackhawk Rd. is crossed by a number of driveways and cross streets. At the same time, the road has a wide shoulder for most of its length, and faster riders may prefer the street to the path.

- At Diffley Rd. (mile 3.3) the bike path switches sides of the street. Jog right across Blackhawk Rd. to continue on the path. A half mile farther on, the trail crosses over I-35E.

- **Watch for this turn:** After crossing over I-35E, the route bends around to pick up the beautiful Highline Trail. The turn from Blackhawk Rd. onto the trail is not obvious. Follow Blackhawk Rd. to the entrance into the Park & Ride, located opposite Beecher Dr. Cross Blackhawk Rd. here and double back on the sidewalk—heading back toward I-35E. Before the bridge, the trail will branch off to your right.

- While a bit tricky to find, the Highline Trail is worth the effort. Lined by city parks and open space, the trail is surrounded by trees, grasses and wildflowers. Following the trail for nearly 4 miles brings you to the rest stop at Trapp Farm Park with its wooded hillsides and views of Schwanz Lake.

Rest Stop ✋: Trapp Farm Park (mile 8), 841 Wilderness Run Road, Eagan, 55123. This woodsy city park is located on the shore of Schwanz Lake and features a large picnic pavilion and an indoor shelter. There is also a playground, restrooms and drinking fountains. In the winter, the city runs a sledding and tubing hill in the park.

- From Trapp Farm Park, follow the bike trail east back to Wilderness Run Rd., then continue to the intersection with Dodd Rd.

- Cross Dodd Rd. and turn left to follow the adjacent trail north to Elrene Rd.

- Turn left onto Elrene Rd., which curves though some of the less densely populated parts of Eagan before intersecting Yankee Doodle Rd.

- Turn left at Yankee Doodle Rd. and follow it to Lexington Ave.

- At Lexington Ave., jog one block north to Northwood Pkwy., then turn left to follow Northwood back to the Community Center. This loop takes you around the back side of the large commercial developments that make up the Eagan Promenade and avoids the heavier traffic along the main drags.

Points of Interest ➜ : The scenic Highline Trail passes through a number of parks, including Downing, Evergreen, Goat Hill, Oak Chase, Oak Pond, Thomas Lake and Walnut Hill. Thomas Lake Park at mile 5.7 makes an excellent alternate rest stop, with large pavilions near the lake shore.

Bridle Ridge Park at mile 10.3 has a playground and a shelter building.

Extended Activities:

- The Blast in the Eagan Community Center (ride start). The Blast is a space-themed indoor playground located in the Eagan Community Center. Visitors can climb through the space shuttle tower and rocket launchpads, explore the Milky Way tunnel, and slide down the gigantic wormhole slide.

Jon's Notes: My first rides through Eagan were on family trips to the Minnesota Zoo in the 1980s. Our route took us down Blackhawk Rd., on the same trail used in this route. The city of Eagan was growing rapidly at that time, and good bike trails have been part of the development plans all along.

What I didn't know about on those early rides to the zoo was the beautiful Highline Trail. The Highline is a multiuse trail with a distinctive character, and it is the centerpiece of this route. The western half of the trail follows a power-line easement and is sandwiched between residential development. This section of the trail is surprisingly varied. In a little under two miles between I-35E and Pilot Knob Rd., the path makes several short but steep climbs as it twists and winds through the narrow greenway. The eastern half of the trail is straighter and flatter, running parallel to Wilderness Run Rd. The whole trail is memorable, and well worth the effort.

Highline Highlights Trail Environment

The "feel" of this route

YELLOW—urban areas or along busy streets

BLUE—suburban areas or neighborhoods

GREEN—parks, parkways and rural or natural settings

GPS Coordinates

- ⊛ Start/End (Central Park): 44° 50' 18.65" N 93° 10' 20.48" W
- 🅟 Rest Stop (Trapp Farm Park): 44° 47' 50.56" N 93° 7' 40.44" W
- → Point of Interest (Thomas Lake Park): 44° 47' 49.53" N   93° 10' 18.54" W
- → Point of Interest (Bridle Ridge Park): 44° 48' 50.81" N   93° 7' 10.89" W

Discover the reclaimed Mississippi riverfront just south of St. Paul

Why Jon Recommends this Ride: This short ride showcases recent work to restore the Mississippi riverfront. The ride begins at an abandoned landfill, which has been reclaimed as a regional park. The ride's turnaround point is a collapsed railroad bridge that has been given new life as a recreational pier. Along the way, it passes through a constantly changing landscape of pristine riverfront, industrial sprawl, and newly created parklands.

Tips: This section of riverfront is continuing to be restored and developed. Keep an eye on this area, and on the Mississippi River Regional Trail south of Heritage Park, as it continues to develop and improve.

Concord by the Mississippi

Length: 12 miles round-trip

Location: South St. Paul, Inver Grove Heights

Terrain: This route is almost completely flat and is a great choice for single-speed bikes and bike trailers.

Considerations: There are few amenities on this ride. Be sure to carry whatever water and snacks you need for the ride, and use the facilities at the Simon's Ravine trailhead before you hit the trail.

Start Location ⭐: Simon's Ravine Trailhead, 1308 Concord St. N, South St. Paul, 55075. Simon's Ravine is a gorge that leads from Concord St. up to Thompson Park at the top of the river bluffs. The trailhead serves both the (very steep) trail up to Thompson Park, and the Mississippi River Regional Trail. The decorative sculpture at the trailhead commemorates the Kaposia Band of Dakota, who had a village at the base of the ravine. Amenities at ride start include free parking, indoor restrooms and drinking fountains.

Connecting Routes in this Book: None.

Route Options: Since this is an out-and-back route, it is easy to shorten the ride by turning back at any time. For a longer ride, continue along the Mississippi River Regional Trail as it follows Concord Blvd. south. The trail currently extends 6 miles to the Rosemount border. Within a few years, the trail is planned to extend all the way to Hastings.

- For a challenging workout, take the trail west from the Simon's Ravine trailhead up the steep river bluff to Thompson County Park. Taking this trail will turn one of the flattest rides in this collection into the hilliest. Just be careful on the ride back down to the parking lot!
- Instead of starting at the Simon's Ravine trailhead, you can begin the ride on the east side of Concord St. at Kaposia Landing Park, 800 Bryant Ave., South St. Paul.

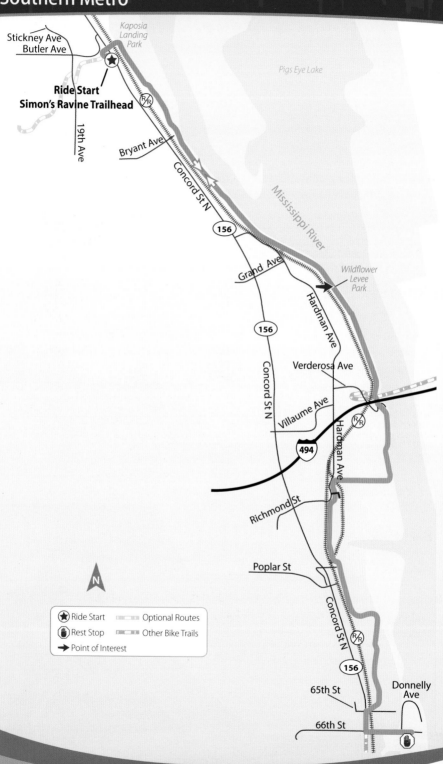

Stickney Ave
Butler Ave

Kaposia
Landing
Park

Pigs Eye Lake

Ride Start
Simon's Ravine Trailhead

19th Ave

Bryant Ave

Concord St N

156

Mississippi River

Grand Ave

Wildflower
Levee
Park

Hardman Ave

156

Verderosa Ave

Concord St N

Villaume Ave

Hardman Ave

494

Richmond St

Poplar St

Concord St N

N

Ride Start   Optional Routes
Rest Stop   Other Bike Trails
Point of Interest

156

65th St   Donnelly
Ave

66th St

Step by Step Directions:

- This ride begins at the Simon's Ravine trailhead, where you can see *Mitakuye Owasin*, a fine example of public sculpture. *Mitakuye Owasin* is Dakota for "all my relations." This sculpture was created by Native American artists Bill La Deaux and Dave Estrada to commemorate the Kaposia Band of Dakota, who lived in this area when European settlers first arrived.

- From the trailhead, the route then crosses over Concord St. to Kaposia Landing Park. Kaposia Landing was built on the site of an abandoned landfill. Little more than a wasteland just a few years ago, the park is just the first example of the exceptional restoration work along this route.

- From Kaposia Landing, follow the Mississippi River Regional Trail south. There are no major trail junctions or spurs along the entire route. You will pass by Wildflower Levee Park at mile 2.3, the I-494 overpass at mile 3.0, and a river overlook at mile 3.5 before curving away from the river.

- The trail jogs west and follows along a rail line before entering Heritage Park. The north end of Heritage Park is undeveloped and being restored to native prairie. Just south of the park is the Rock Island Swing Bridge recreational pier, the turnaround point for the ride.

Rest Stop (✋)**:** Swing Bridge Park (at mile 6.1), 4465 66th St., Inver Grove Heights, 55077. The Rock Island Swing Bridge served as an important river crossing from 1895 to 1999. The western span now serves as a recreational pier. Amenities include indoor restrooms, drinking fountains, a picnic shelter, picnic tables and a bike repair station.

- The return trip follows the Mississippi River Regional Trail back north to Kaposia Landing and Simon's Ravine trailhead, once again passing the river overlook, the I-494 overpass, and Wildflower Levee Park.

Point of Interest ➔ **:** Check out *The Industrious Cooperative Ant* sculpture in Wildflower Levee Park (at mile 2.3, and 8.4 on the return trip). This sculpture by Rabi Sanfo is in many ways symbolic of this entire route. Rabi created this sculpture out of scrap metal he recovered while volunteering on cleanup projects along the Mississippi River floodplain. What was once an eyesore along the banks of the Mighty Miss has become something for folks to enjoy along the reclaimed riverfront.

Extended Activities: None.

Jon's Notes: In the 1990s, I used to ride across the aged Rock Island Swing Bridge and up Concord St. with my cycling club. The bridge was built in 1895 and became a toll bridge in the early 1980s. The toll for cars was 75 cents. When we rolled up on our bikes, the bridge operator charged us just 10 cents apiece. The bridge's impressive wrought iron frame supported two decks, which overlooked a mixture of industry and natural riverfront. The upper deck was once used by trains, while the wood-covered lower deck was used by cars and the occasional bicycle.

From the bridge, we would ride back toward St. Paul along Concord St. Though designated as a bike route, there was no bike trail, and Concord had only a narrow shoulder. But in a few places, like the south end of Pigs Eye Lake, Concord would pass close to the river and we might catch sight of a bald eagle perched along the far shore.

When we rode on it, the century-old bridge had clearly seen better days. The rusting girders of the eastern span looked like they could topple into the river at almost any moment. And in 2008, nine years after being closed to traffic, that is exactly what happened.

While the eastern span is gone, the western span has found new life as a recreational pier. Cleaned up and reinforced, its two decks still overlook an engaging mixture of industry and natural riverfront. Meanwhile, the bike route has moved off of Concord and onto a new trail that tracks close to the river for most of its length.

Concord by the Mississippi Trail Environment

The "feel" of this route

YELLOW—urban areas or along busy streets
BLUE—suburban areas or neighborhoods
GREEN—parks, parkways and rural or natural settings

GPS Coordinates

- Start/End (Simon's Ravine Trailhead): 44° 54' 45.46" N
  93° 3' 12.79" W
- Turnaround/Rest Stop (Heritage Park): 44° 51' 11.83" N
  93° 0' 36.79" W
- → Point of Interest (Wildflower Levee Park): 44° 53' 31.19" N
  93° 1' 26.35" W

A challenging but rewarding ride that climbs the bluffs and hills above the Minnesota River

Why Jon Recommends this Ride: Mendota Heights is aptly named. It is one of the hillier parts of the Twin Cities, rising away from the confluence of the Minnesota and Mississippi Rivers. It also has an excellent network of local bike trails, and hosts most of the splendid Big Rivers Regional Trail. This ride scales the heights of Mendota Heights and twists and winds around some of the community's many parks. It also passes through the historic township of Mendota, which is home to some of the oldest buildings in Minnesota.

Tips: This is one of the trickier routes in the collection. The route is both hilly and sometimes complicated. Keep your map handy and give extra attention to the directions.

Length: 13.5 miles, with options of 11.9 miles, 12.5 miles and 12.9 miles

Location: Mendota Heights, Mendota, Lilydale

Terrain: Fairly hilly; long, steady grades and some significant hills.

Considerations: The turn onto the bike trail at the top of Lilydale Rd. (mile 9.5) is easy to miss. Keep a close eye on the map and watch for a gate on your left shortly before the top of the hill. Go around the gate on the right side to get on the trail.

The trail past the gate at Lilydale Rd. is winding, has a few steep descents and passes through the woods. Use caution, especially in the fall when the trail can become covered with leaves.

Start Location ⭐: Mendakota Park, 2000 Mendakota Dr., Mendota Heights, 55120. The centerpiece of this city park is a set of four baseball and softball fields, but the park also features parking, a playground, restrooms, drinking fountains and picnic facilities as well. There is a small concessions stand in the middle of the baseball complex that may be open during games.

Connecting Routes in this Book:

Circling the Fort (page 14) shares a segment.

Route Options:

11.9 miles To avoid one of the steepest hills on the route, stay right at the trail junction next to the picnic shelter at mile 10.5. Cross under Marie Ave., follow the trail south toward Mendota Rd./Hwy. 110, then turn left and continue to Dodd Rd. to rejoin the main route.

12.5 miles For a slightly shorter route, continue straight on Mendota Heights Rd. at mile 4.3. (Note: there is no bike path along this stretch of road). Follow Mendota Heights Rd. across Hwy. 13 to rejoin the main route at the Mendota Overlook.

12.9 miles You can also begin the ride in the shopping area parking lot on the southeast corner of Dodd Rd. and Hwy. 110. Another option is to begin at The Village, located on Dodd Rd., just north of Hwy. 110.

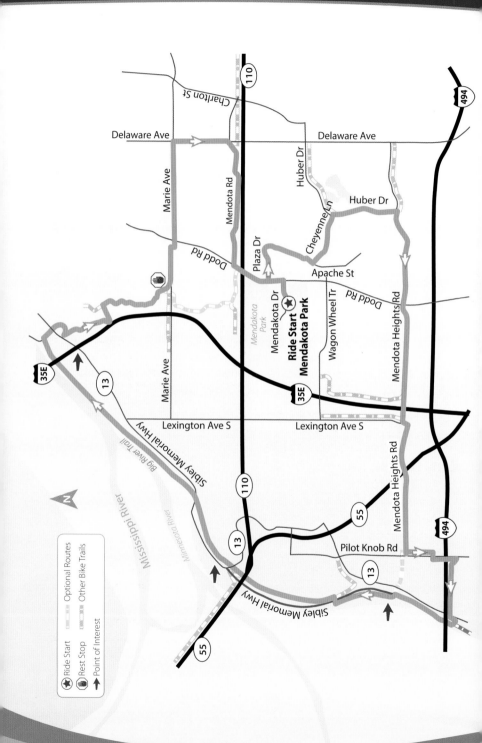

Step by Step Directions:

- Begin by following Mendakota Dr. east out of the park, then jog a short distance north along Dodd Rd. before turning east again along Plaza Dr.

- In about two blocks, Plaza Dr. dead-ends and is replaced with a bike path that follows along the edge of Friendly Marsh Park. At the southeast corner of the park, the bike trail empties out onto Apache St. Follow Apache St. south to Cheyenne Ln.

- Turn left onto Cheyenne Ln. and follow it to the intersection with Huber Ln. Cross Huber Ln. and turn right onto the adjacent bike trail. Follow the trail south to Mendota Heights Rd.

- After crossing Mendota Heights Rd., turn right onto the bike trail. The route follows the bike trails along Mendota Heights Rd. for 2.5 miles to Pilot Knob Rd. The trail crosses Mendota Heights Rd. twice. Jog right at Dodd Rd., and jog left at Lexington Ave., just after crossing over I-35E.

- **Watch for this turn:** At Pilot Knob Rd., turn left and follow the bike path two blocks to the first traffic light. At the light, jog across Pilot Knob Rd., then continue south on the bike path to cross over I-494 before turning right onto the bike trail along the freeway.

- This trail continues along the I-494 bridge all the way across the Mississippi River Valley, but our route takes a left turn onto the ramp off the bridge after crossing over Hwy. 13, well before the river.

- The ramp takes you down to the Big Rivers Regional Trail, which parallels Hwy. 13. About a half mile up the trail is the Mendota Overlook, which offers a spectacular view of the Minnesota River valley from the historic Stone Overlook Wall.

- A mile and a half farther along, the trail passes through the tiny city of Mendota, which is home to some of the oldest buildings in the state, including the Church of St. Peter and the Sibley House.

- Big Rivers Regional Trail ends at Lilydale Rd., next to a wooden railroad bridge. Cross over Lilydale Rd., then turn right on the bike trail and follow it up the hill as the road curves to the right. This is one of the most substantial climbs along the ride.

- **Watch for this turn:** As the road straightens out near the top of the climb, the route turns left onto a beautiful, wooded bike trail. The unpaved entrance to this trail is gated to keep cars out, and it is very easy to overlook. Keep an eye out for the trail entrance on the left-hand side. If you reach Sibley Memorial Hwy. (Hwy. 13) at the top of Lilydale Rd., you have gone just a bit too far. When you first spot the trail, it may appear to be closed, but you will see the well-worn path on the right side of the gate for bikes. Use some caution here as the passage on the right of the gate is narrow.

- Follow this local trail though the woods, taking a right turn at the "T" intersection, to get to the picnic shelter at Valley Park.

Rest Stop 🖐: Valley Park, 821 Marie Ave. W, Mendota Heights, 55118. This city park (located at mile 10.5) sits on the border between a wooded corridor and a suburban neighborhood. Amenities at the rest stop include portable latrines, a picnic shelter and a playground.

- From the picnic shelter, turn left, cross over the wooden footbridge, and cut through the parking lot to get on a bike trail along Marie Ave. The bike trail follows Marie Ave. for nearly a mile, almost all of it uphill, to Delaware St. and the campus of Sibley High School.
- Turn right at Delaware Ave. to ride around the high school and back down the hill to the Hwy. 110 Frontage Rd.
- Turn right on the bike path along the frontage road to head back toward Dodd Rd.
- A left turn along Dodd takes you across Mendota Rd./Hwy. 110, south to Plaza Dr. where you can retrace your steps the two remaining blocks to Mendakota Park.

Points of Interest ➔ : The highlight of the Mendota Overlook (mile 5.7) is the Stone Overlook Wall. Built in 1938 by the WPA, this overlook continues to offer spectacular views of the Minnesota River Valley.

Minnesota's oldest church, the Church of St. Peter's, is located just off the route at mile 7.0. After crossing under the Mendota Bridge (Hwy. 55), turn left onto the bike path and follow it about two blocks northeast to the church's entrance along Sibley Memorial Hwy. The original church, built in 1853, is located in the far corner of the grounds, behind the newer buildings.

There is a Holiday gas station near the top of Lilydale Rd. at mile 9.5, about three blocks off the route. This can be a convenient stop if you need a restroom or a quick snack. To get there, follow the trail all the way up Lilydale Rd., then along Hwy. 13 for a block and a half. Cross Hwy. 13 at the crosswalk, then turn left onto the sidewalk to take the bridge over I-35E to the store.

Extended Activities:
- Sibley House Historic Site (mile 7.3). Henry Hastings Sibley was the regional manager of the American Fur Company and the first governor of Minnesota. The Minnesota Historical Society has restored his original stone house and opens it to visitors on summer weekends. To get there from the bike route, turn left on D Street at mile 7.3 and follow it for three short blocks across Hwy. 13 and around the bend.

Jon's Notes: There is no doubt about it, this is one of the most challenging rides in the book. This is a complex route, so you will want to keep a close eye on the map and directions. It is also the hilliest ride in the collection. Back in the 1990s, several of my cycling club's regular training routes passed through Mendota Heights. We were looking for steep hills that would give us a good workout, and this is one area where we could find them in abundance. One thing we found tricky, however, was connecting the best roads and trails together on our routes. We would often end up riding along busy sections of Highways 13 and 55. These were not the best connections, but the rides were always worth the trouble. Today, Mendota Heights offers an ever-improving selection of bike trails, including the excellent Big Rivers Regional Trail. The area is still full of hills, and there are still some tricky connections on this route. But just as we did years ago on our club rides, I think you will find the challenges well worth the effort.

Scaling the Heights Trail Environment

The "feel" of this route
YELLOW—urban areas or along busy streets
BLUE—suburban areas or neighborhoods
GREEN—parks, parkways and rural or natural settings

GPS Coordinates
- ⊛ Start/End (Mendakota Park): 44° 52' 42.11" N 93° 7' 47.10" W
- ⊚ Rest Stop (Valley View Park): 44° 53' 28.86" N 93° 7' 39.62" W
- → Point of Interest (Mendota Overlook): 44° 52' 2.04" N   93° 10' 24.75" W
- → Point of Interest (St. Peter's Church): 44° 53' 5.76" N   93° 10' 6.41" W
- → Point of Interest (Holiday gas station): 44° 54' 0.57" N   93° 8' 14.35" W

One of the flattest, smoothest, most popular trails in the Twin Cities

Why Jon Recommends this Ride: Starting from the Minneapolis Sculpture Garden, this ride heads out to Hopkins and back on some of the flattest, widest, smoothest bike trails in the Twin Cities. This route is a superb choice for trailers and single-speed bikes.

Tips: Instead of parking in the pay lot next to the Sculpture Garden, you can park for free three blocks away next to Parade Ice Arena at 600 Kenwood Pkwy.

Length: 14 miles, with options of 5.5 miles and 14 miles-plus

Location: Minneapolis, St. Louis Park, Hopkins

Terrain: Smooth and flat with no significant hills.

Considerations: There are a number of crisscrossing bike trails near the beginning and end of the route. Be sure not to miss the turn off of the Cedar Lake Trail on your way back to the Sculpture Garden.

This is a popular trail and is heavily used by fast cyclists, joggers, dog walkers and inline skaters. Most of the trail is quite wide, allowing ample room to pass, but it may become congested at times.

Start Location ⭐: Minneapolis Sculpture Garden, 726 Vineland Pl., Minneapolis, 55403. The Sculpture Garden is a free open-air museum and home to the iconic *Spoonbridge and Cherry*. Amenities at the ride start include pay parking, drinking fountains, restrooms and public art. Free parking is available at the nearby Parade Ice Arena.

Connecting Routes in this Book:

Trails to Light Rails (page 38) shares a segment.

Midtown Lollipop (page 26) comes within a few blocks.

Trails to Rails (page 74) shares a segment.

Route Options:

5.5 miles For a shorter, 5.5-mile ride, turn south off the Cedar Lake Trail at mile 1.6 to circle Cedar Lake and return along the KenilworthTrail.

14 miles-plus To extend the route, ride out-and-back along the Minnesota River Bluffs Regional Trail from The Depot Coffee Shop at mile 7.1.

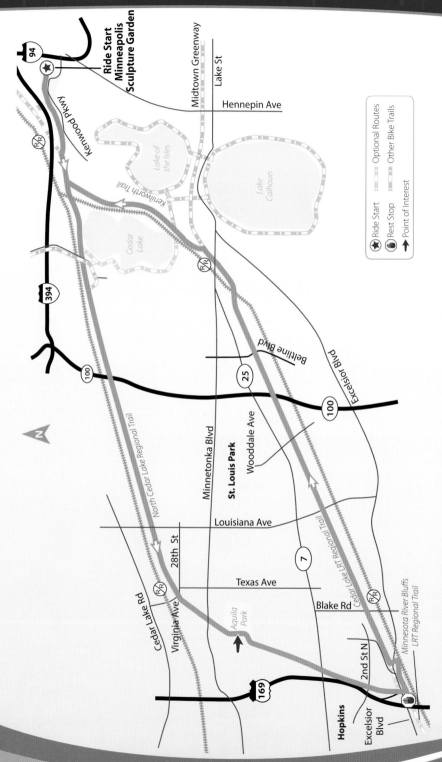

Ride Start
Minneapolis
Sculpture Garden

94

Midtown Greenway

Lake St

Hennepin Ave

Kenwood Pkwy

Lake of
the Isles

Lake
Calhoun

Kenilworth Trail

Cedar
Lake

394

100

Betline Blvd

25

100

Excelsior Blvd

N

North Cedar Lake Regional Trail

Minnetonka Blvd

St. Louis Park

Wooddale Ave

Louisiana Ave

28th St

7

Texas Ave

Cedar Lake Rd

Virginia Ave

Aquila
Park

Blake Rd

Cedar Lake LRT Regional Trail

Minnesota River Bluffs
LRT Regional Trail

2nd St N

169

Hopkins

Excelsior
Blvd

Ride Start
Rest Stop
Point of Interest
Optional Routes
Other Bike Trails

Step by Step Directions:

- From the sculpture garden, follow the sidewalk/bike trail west along Kenwood Pkwy.

- **Watch for this turn:** As Kenwood Pkwy. curves away from the freeway wall, turn right onto the spur trail that connects to the Cedar Lake Trail. Do not take the right-most path here, which goes up to the freeway bridge and crosses over the Cedar Lake Trail.

- After a few hundred yards, jog right, across the railroad tracks, to follow the northern branch of the Cedar Lake Trail past the north end of Cedar Lake.

- The trail continues west along the railroad tracks for a bit over 3 miles before curving south toward Aquila Park.

- Turn right at Aquila Park to stay on the Cedar Lake Trail and follow it to Excelsior Blvd. The rest stop at The Depot Coffee Shop is located on the south side of Excelsior Blvd.

Rest Stop ✋: The Depot Coffee House (mile 6.9), 9451 Excelsior Blvd., Hopkins, 55343. Located right on a bike trail, the Depot caters especially to cyclists. They have plenty of outdoor seating, offer a great selection of hot and cold drinks, and are happy to fill your bike bottle up with ice water free of charge. While you are there, take a look at their upcoming concerts—they have great live music in the summertime. Amenities at the rest stop include water (fill up inside), restrooms, picnic tables, and indoor seating for customers.

- From the Depot, ride a block east to the intersection of Excelsior and Jackson. Cross both streets at the large intersection to pick up the southern branch of the Cedar Lake Trail back toward Minneapolis. This segment of the Cedar Lake Trail is even wider and smoother than the northern branch.

- After about 4 miles, the trail branches. Turn left at this junction to get on the Kenilworth Trail. The other branch continues straight toward Lake Canhoun, where it becomes the Midtown Greenway.

- The Kenilworth Trail continues north for 1.5 miles through a wide swath of urban woods before intersecting the northern branch of the Cedar Lake Trail close to the I-394 overpass.

- Shortly after joining up with the Cedar Lake Trail, and before crossing under I-394, take the trail exit on the right and follow the spur back to Kenwood Pkwy.

- Turn left onto the trail along Kenwood Pkwy. and follow it back to the sculpture garden.

Point of Interest ➜ : Aquila Park (mile 5.3) has restrooms and a drinking fountain.

Extended Activities: There are a number of great family activities available right at the ride start.

- The Minneapolis Sculpture Garden is a joint project of the Walker Art Center and the Minneapolis Park and Recreation Board. The largest urban sculpture garden in the country, it covers 11 acres and features more than 40 works of art and a botanical conservatory. Admission to the garden and conservatory is free.

- The Walker Art Center is the oldest public art gallery in the Upper Midwest. Recently expanded, it continues to carry on its tradition of promoting artistic creativity and active engagement with modern visual, performing and media arts.

- Parade Ice Arena offers a few hours of public ice skating and skate rental throughout the summer.

Jon's Notes: The Cedar Lake Trail forms a large oval, with a southern and a northern branch, that stretches from the edge of downtown Minneapolis out to Hopkins. Following old railroad grades for most of the route, the trail is one of the widest, smoothest and flattest rides in the metro area. The Minneapolis Sculpture Garden and downtown skyline provide a picturesque backdrop for the ride start, but you quickly leave the city behind as you head out on the trail.

This is a terrific ride to take with young children. The route is flat enough to be easy for youth on single-speed bikes or adults pulling loaded trailers. There are relatively few road crossings, and most of the trails are wide enough to allow users to pass easily.

Cedar Lake Express Trail Environment

The "feel" of this route

YELLOW—urban areas or along busy streets

BLUE—suburban areas or neighborhoods

GREEN—parks, parkways and rural or natural settings

GPS Coordinates

⊛ Start/End (Minneapolis Sculpture Garden): 44° 58' 11.89" N   93° 17' 20.67 "W

◉ Rest Stop (The Depot Coffee House): 44° 55' 25.97" N   93° 23' 55.79" W

➜ Point of Interest: (Aquila Park): 44° 56' 41.88" N   93° 23' 22.11" W

Miles of traffic-free riding through woods and fields, just minutes from downtown

Why Jon Recommends this Ride:
Elm Creek Park is the largest park in Hennepin County's Three Rivers Park District. The park contains over 20 miles of paved trails, including the large outer loop described here. This ride will take you through shaded woods, over wooden bridges that cross creeks, and across rolling stretches of tallgrass prairie filled with songbirds and other wildlife. The entire route is along smooth, wide, well-maintained trails away from roads and traffic. As you circle around this beautiful park, it is easy to forget how close you are to downtown Minneapolis.

Tips:
There are no places to stop for drinking water on the northern loop of this ride. Be sure to carry whatever you need with you.

Elm Creek Park

Length: 15 miles, with options of 5 miles and 7.5 miles

Location: Maple Grove, Dayton, Champlin (but all of it is inside Elm Creek Park)

Terrain: Rolling terrain with a few short but steep slopes on the second half of the route.

Considerations: There are a number of trail junctions along the route, some of which take you out of the park into the surrounding neighborhoods. Most important junctions feature maps, but it's a good idea to keep this book handy.

The route crosses over a few boardwalks and wooden bridges, which can be slippery when wet. Use extra caution if you go riding during or shortly after a rain.

The last third of the ride is the hilliest. Be sure to save some energy for the end!

Start Location ★: Elm Creek Park Reserve general recreation area, 12400 James Deane Pkwy., Maple Grove, 55369. The general recreation area has a large parking lot, and it hosts most of the park's summertime amenities. Amenities at ride start include restrooms, drinking fountains, picnic facilities, a swimming pond, play areas and volleyball courts. There is also a seasonal concessions stand at the swimming pond.

Connecting Routes in this Book:

Rush Creek Lollipop (page 56) shares short segments.

Route Options:

5 miles Turn right at the trail junction at mile 1.8 and follow the small trail loop back to the start.

7.5 miles Continue straight at the "T" junction near the Eastman Nature Center to complete the small loop back to the start.

For a longer ride, add either of the shorter loops to the large loop.

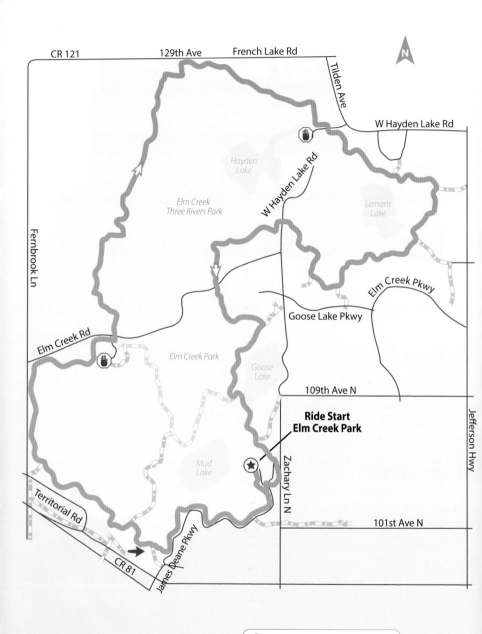

CR 121   129th Ave   French Lake Rd

Tilden Ave

W Hayden Lake Rd

Fernbrook Ln

Hayden Lake

Elm Creek Three Rivers Park

W Hayden Lake Rd

Lemans Lake

Elm Creek Pkwy

Elm Creek Rd

Goose Lake Pkwy

Elm Creek Park

Goose Lake

109th Ave N

Ride Start Elm Creek Park

Zachary Ln N

Mud Lake

Jefferson Hwy

Territorial Rd

101st Ave N

CR 81

James Deane Pkwy

⬤ Ride Start   ▢▢▢ Optional Routes
🖐 Rest Stop   ▢▢▢ Other Bike Trails
➡ Point of Interest

Step by Step Directions:

- This ride begins at the general recreation area in Elm Creek Park. From the parking lot, the route heads out toward James Dean Pkwy., then turns right onto the bike trail. The trail parallels the road as it winds its way back toward the park entrance, passing by the disc golf course, winter recreation area, and the historic Pierre Bottineau House before curving west, away from the street.

- Shortly after leaving James Dean Pkwy. behind, the route comes to its first major trail junction. A left turn here takes you on the outer loop around the park, and brings you by the brand new Eastman Nature Center. Located about a quarter mile south of the bike trail, the nature center is a great place to stop and explore.

Rest Stop 1 (✋): The Eastman Nature Center (mile 4.5), 13351 Elm Creek Rd., Dayton, 55369. This is a brand new nature center that provides a wide variety of exhibits and activities. Amenities include restrooms, a cafe and a drinking fountain.

- Just past the driveway to the nature center, the route turns left and crosses Elm Creek Road to stay on the outer trail loop. If you stop at the nature center and depart along the bike path, rather than the driveway, you will need to backtrack slightly to stay on the outer loop. Check the map, and keep an eye on the maps located at most major trail junctions in the park.

- The trail immediately north of Elm Creek Road moves across open grassland and savanna for a half mile before descending to a 250-yard-long boardwalk over a wooded wetland. After another half mile, the trail emerges into the open again and continues winding along the western, then northern, edges of the park. This stretch is the flattest section of the ride. There is a pit stop available at the Hayden Lake Road parking area, near the halfway point for the ride, with latrines but no running water.

Rest Stop 2 (✋): Hayden Lake Trail parking lot (mile 8.3). Located at the western end of W. Hayden Lake Rd., Champlin, 55316. This trailhead, located near the north end of the park, provides latrines but has few other amenities.

- From the Hayden Lake Trail parking area, the route swings out into the easternmost parts of the park before turning south again to head back toward the ride start. This is the hilliest section of the route, and it also takes the trail closest to some of the suburban development just outside the park. The few intersecting trails along this stretch all lead out into the surrounding neighborhoods.

- Near the south end of Goose Lake, make a left-hand turn at the "T" intersection. A mile later, the trail crosses over James Dean Pkwy., just before the driveway back to the general recreation area.

Point of Interest →: The Pierre Bottineau House Historic Landmark (mile 1.4). This house was built in 1854, four years before Minnesota became a state. It was the first house in the area and has been moved at least three times before finally becoming a historic landmark here in Elm Creek Park.

Extended Activities:

- Elm Creek Park (ride start). This is a gem of the Hennepin County Three Rivers Park District. It encompasses 4,900 acres in the northwest metro and features a variety of amenities for recreation and ways to connect with nature. The general recreation area located on James Dean Pkwy. has picnic areas, and is equipped with volleyball courts, a swimming pond and a large children's play area. There is also a disc golf course just a short distance away. Located at the ride start, Elm Creek's man-made swimming pond features filtered, chlorinated water and a sandy beach. There is a small user fee.

- Eastman Nature Center (Rest Stop 1). This is a new, 13,000-square-foot nature center that is tucked in the woods just off of the bike trail on the west side of the park. The center features indoor exhibits, outdoor viewing areas and a small cafe. Activities include self-guided nature hikes with audio stops (playable on a cell phone), and an outdoor children's nature exploration area.

Jon's Notes: Riding through Elm Creek Park feels like going back to a time when pristine prairie, savanna and wetlands still dotted the landscape around the Twin Cities. The park feels truly wild in places and is home to a diversity of wildlife, including sandhill cranes, eagles, trumpeter swans, deer and beaver.

I usually bike to Elm Creek Park if I am going to ride there. The trip takes me through the variety of urban and suburban landscapes that make up the Twin Cities. But all of that drops away when I get into the park. Although the suburban development is never far away, it is hidden by the rolling hills and patchy woods of the park. I find myself taking in more of the surroundings and seeing things that I might easily ride past on a more developed trail. On a recent trip through the park, I found myself drawn to the diversity of animal tracks on the dirt path. There, mixed in with the prints of several domestic dogs, were the unmistakably narrow, precise tracks of a coyote.

When I finish a ride though Elm Creek Park, my mind is at ease. I feel both relaxed and alert, a feeling that easily carries me the whole ride home.

Elm Creek Park Trail Environment

The "feel" of this route

YELLOW—urban areas or along busy streets

BLUE—suburban areas or neighborhoods

GREEN—parks, parkways and rural or natural settings

GPS Coordinates

- ⊛ Start/End (Elm Creek Park): 45° 8' 28.42" N 93° 25' 27.03" W
- ⊕ Rest Stop 1 (Eastman Nature Center): 45° 9' 16.49" N 93° 26' 59.72" W
- ⊕ Rest Stop 2 (Hayden Lake Trail): 45° 9' 28.56" N 93° 24' 56.39" W
- → Point of Interest (Pierre Bottineau House Historic Landmark): 45° 8' 6.71" N 93° 26' 34.13" W

Pedal along the shores of the area's second-largest lake

Why Jon Recommends this Ride: This ride circles around the city of Plymouth and follows the Medicine Lake Trail, the Luce Line Trail, and local bike paths. The ride begins and ends in the beautiful Clifton E. French Regional Park on the shores of Medicine Lake, the second-largest lake in the Twin Cities metro area. French Park is a recent addition to the Three Rivers Park District and is named in honor of the district's first superintendent whose farsighted development planning preserved more than 24,000 acres in Hennepin County as public parklands.

Tips: Be sure to save some energy for the end of the ride. The last third of the route is the hilliest part.

Length: 15 miles, with options of 7.5 miles and 15 miles-plus

Location: Plymouth

Terrain: Flat to rolling terrain with a few moderate hills.

Considerations: The multiuse trail along the east shore of Medicine Lake is hilly, winding and narrow in some places. Use caution—and use your brakes.

There are two boardwalks of a few hundred yards each along the Luce Line trail near mile 3.5. These wooden surfaces can be slippery when they are wet. Use extra caution if you ride during, or shortly after, a rain.

Use caution at the large, busy intersection of Vicksburg Ln. and Hwy. 55 (mile 9.2).

Start Location ⭐: Clifton E. French Regional Park, 12605 Rockford Road, Plymouth, 55441. Located on the north shore of Medicine Lake, French Park offers a wide variety of outdoor recreational activities. The park has a swimming beach, a fishing pier, extensive picnic grounds, free parking, restrooms, and a large multilevel outdoor playground. There is also a concessions stand in the visitor center that sells snack food and treats.

Connecting Routes in this Book: None.

Route Options:

7.5 miles For a shorter ride, turn right onto the bike trail along West Medicine Lake Dr. at mile 3.9 and follow it north to the intersection with Rockford Rd. This route features a rest area at West Medicine Lake Park at mile 4.4.

15 miles-plus For a longer ride, adventurous riders may want to explore the Luce Line State Trail, a crushed limestone trail that extends far past Parkers Lake into the western prairie.

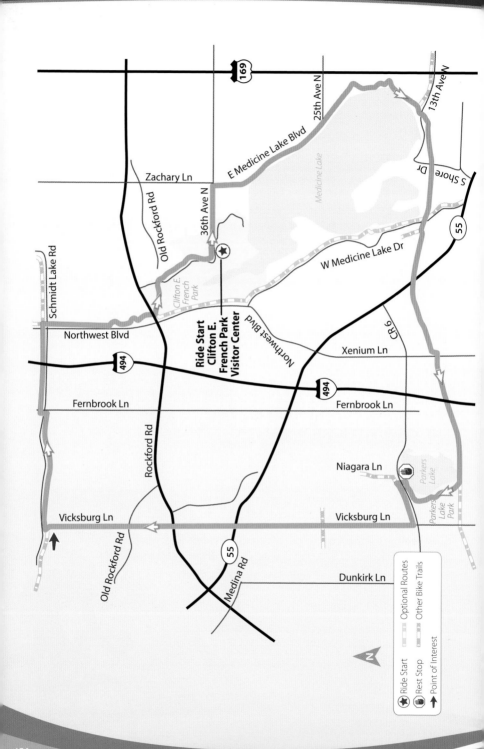

169

25th Ave N

13th Ave N

E Medicine Lake Blvd

Zachary Ln

Old Rockford Rd

36th Ave N

Medicine Lake

S Shore Dr

55

W Medicine Lake Dr

Schmidt Lake Rd

Clifton E. French Park

Ride Start Clifton E. French Park Visitor Center

Northwest Blvd

494

Northwest Blvd

Xenium Ln

CR 6

494

Fernbrook Ln

Fernbrook Ln

Rockford Rd

Niagara Ln

Parkers Lake

Vicksburg Ln

Old Rockford Rd

55

Medina Rd

Vicksburg Ln

Parkers Lake Park

Dunkirk Ln

N

★ Ride Start   Optional Routes
🚏 Rest Stop   Other Bike Trails
↑ Point of Interest

Step by Step Directions:

- The ride begins at the French Park visitor center. From the visitor center parking lot, head east on the bike path for a very short distance to the first crosswalk.
- Jog left across road to follow the Medicine Lake Regional Trail out of the park.
- The trail follows 36th Ave. for a few blocks before turning right along East Medicine Lake Blvd., which it follows for the length of the lake.
- At the southern end of the lake, the route intersects the Luce Line Regional Trail and makes a right turn to follow it to the west. Shortly after getting on the Luce Line Trail, the route crosses over the marshy wetlands south of Medicine Lake via a pair of long wooden boardwalks. The route continues west through neighborhoods, light industrial zones and wooded corridors to the south end of Parkers Lake.
- **Watch for this turn:** The route leaves the Luce Line Trail less than half a mile before the blacktop ends. If you reach Shenandoah Ln., you have overshot it by about 100 yards.
- Follow the trail around Parkers Lake to the rest stop.

Rest Stop (✋): Parkers Lake Park (mile 6.9), 15205 County Rd. 6, Plymouth, 55447. This park wraps around the north and west shores of Parkers Lake. Most of the park's amenities are located on the north shore, near the visitor center. Amenities include picnic facilities, a playground, a swimming area, indoor restrooms, and a drinking fountain. In addition: a seasonal concessions stand in the visitor center sells snacks and treats.

- From the rest area at Parkers Lake Park, our route ducks under County Rd. 6. You will find a tunnel under the road just east of the visitor center. After passing through the tunnel, curve around to the left to come back up to street level, then turn right onto the bike trail along County Rd. 6.
- Follow the trail along County Rd. 6 west to Vicksburg Ln. Cross Vicksburg, then turn right onto the adjacent path. Be careful making this turn, especially if you are towing a trailer. The angle of the curb-cut and the placement of the traffic light make this a very tight turn.
- Follow Vicksburg Ln. north for a little over 3 miles to the tiny Gateway Park.
- Turn right to follow the trail along Schmidt Lake Rd. back to the east. At Fernbrook Ln. the trail jogs left across Schmidt Lake Rd.

- After passing under I-494, the route makes another right turn at Northwest Blvd., which is also County Rd. 61. The trail follows Northwest Blvd. for a little over half a mile before curving gently away from the street. A bit farther along, it crosses underneath Rockford Rd. and re-enters French Park.

- After crossing two park roads, the route takes a final right turn at a trail junction to return to the visitor center.

Point of Interest ➔ : The Gateway Neighborhood Playground at Vicksburg Ln. and Schmidt Lake Rd. (mile 10.9) offers a nice, shaded spot to rest.

Extended Activities:

- French Park (ride start) is a great place to spend a summer day with the family. Some of the activities available at the park include:

- Geocaching: The visitor center loans out GPS units at no cost, allowing visitors to experience this high-tech treasure hunt in the park.

- Swimming: The swimming area on Medicine Lake features a large sand beach, umbrellas, volleyball courts and nearby picnic grounds. It's a great place to spend a hot summer's day.

- Paddling: Medicine Lake is a beautiful lake to explore in a small boat. Canoes, kayaks, paddleboats and rowboats are available for rent next to the swimming beach.

- Playground: French Park features a large, multilevel play structure outside of the visitor center. Kids of all ages can enjoy climbing through the structure's maze of cargo nets, or digging in the nearby sandbox.

- Outdoor Recreation School: French Park is also home to the Three River's Park District's Outdoor Recreation School. The school, located at the Field Operation Center north of the visitor center, offers a wide range of programs and activities and features a 25' climbing wall. Be sure to call ahead to check hours and available programs: (763) 694-7717.

Jon's Notes: The city of Plymouth boasts about 130 miles of multiuse trails. Some of the highlights of this trail network include the Luce Line Trail and the Medicine Lake Trail, which together form nearly half of this route.

The Luce Line Trail follows an old railroad grade that once ran from Minneapolis to the tiny township of Gluek, near Montevideo. The line was originally built by William Luce and his son in 1908, under the banner of the Electric Short Line Railroad Company. Their goal was to extend the line out to Billings, South Dakota. The project failed in 1927 and the line changed hands many times over the following decades. In 1970, the portion of the line west of Vicksburg Ln. was abandoned. This corridor later became the Luce Line State Trail—a limestone-and-gravel surface trail that stretches 63 miles from Plymouth into the Minnesota prairie. The eastern section of the line is now owned by Union Pacific and is still in operation. The Luce Line Regional Trail parallels the active rail corridor for most of its 9-mile length between Minneapolis and Plymouth. Although an active rail corridor, the Luce Line sees little traffic. In all my rides along the trail, I have never seen a train. In between sections of suburban development, you'll find stretches of wetlands just south of Medicine Lake. These sections are particularly vibrant in the springtime when red-winged blackbirds are staking out their territories.

The Medicine Lake Regional Trail is part of the expanding network of trails managed by Hennepin County's Three Rivers Park District. The trail passes through French Park and follows along the eastern shore of Medicine Lake— offering great views and access to two of the lake's public beaches. There is another segment of the Medicine Lake Regional Trail that runs south out of Elm Creek Park. When the trail is complete, it will connect the Luce Line Trail to the Rush Creek Trail and the trail networks of Elm Creek Park.

Good Medicine Trail Environment

The "feel" of this route

YELLOW—urban areas or along busy streets
BLUE—suburban areas or neighborhoods
GREEN—parks, parkways and rural or natural settings

GPS Coordinates

✱ Start/End (Clifton E. French Regional Park): 45° 1' 18.29" N 93° 26' 1.98" W

⦿ Rest Stop (Parkers Lake Park): 44° 59' 42.39" N   93° 28' 38.04" W

→ Point of Interest (Gateway Neighborhood Playground): 45° 2' 36.60" N   93° 28' 56.55" W

Enjoy the parks and trails of one of the "Best Places to Live in the U.S."

Why Jon Recommends this Ride:

Eden Prairie has one of the best networks of multiuse trails in the metro area. No wonder *Money* magazine named the city the "Best Place to Live" in the U.S. in 2010. From the wetlands around Purgatory Creek and the wooded shores of Staring Lake to Flying Cloud Airport and the historic Dorenkemper House in Riley Lake Park, this ride, like Eden Prairie, has something for everyone.

Tips:

There isn't anywhere to buy food near the rest stop, so pack a snack if you want one. If you forget, you could stop at the convenience store at Valley View Rd. and Eden Prairie Rd., across the street from Round Lake Park (mile 3.3).

Length: 14 miles, with options of 6 miles, 13 miles, and 14 miles-plus

Location: Eden Prairie

Terrain: Hilly. Several long, steady grades and some steep hills.

Considerations: Around mile 4, the trail narrows and there are a number of residential streets crossing the trail past Round Lake. More experienced riders may prefer to follow the low-traffic road along this section.

There are also several significant hills on this ride, including a steep downhill in Staring Lake Park at mile 11.

Start Location ★: Purgatory Creek Park, 13001 Technology Dr., Eden Prairie, 55344. This park is located along the edge of a large wetland along Purgatory Creek. Amenities at the ride start include parking, a drinking fountain, indoor restrooms and a picnic shelter. There are a half-dozen restaurants located across the street from the park, many of which feature views of the wetland. Park highlights include a small gazebo, a large fountain in the creek, and the Eden Prairie Veterans Memorial.

Connecting Routes in this Book: None.

Route Options:

6 miles For a short "dumbbell" route that avoids the hills, turn left on the bike path just before the Optima business complex at mile 0.4 and follow it south along Purgatory Creek to Staring Lake. Circle around Staring Lake and return to Purgatory Creek Park along the main route. This is a great route for young kids.

13 miles To skip the rest area and shorten the ride slightly, continue straight at the intersection with the Minnesota River Bluffs Regional Trail at mile 7.3, then turn left onto Pioneer Trail to rejoin the main route.

14 miles-plus For a longer ride, adventurous cyclists may enjoy riding out-and-back on the gravel-surfaced Minnesota River Bluffs Regional Trail.

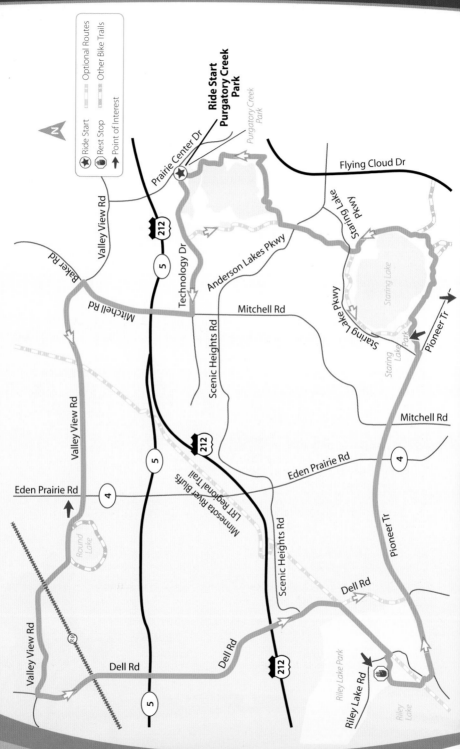

**Ride Start
Purgatory Creek
Park**

Step by Step Directions:

- From Purgatory Creek Park, follow the bike trail west along Technology Dr.
- Turn right to follow the trail along Mitchell Rd. north to Valley View Rd.
- Turn left at Valley View Rd. to follow the adjacent trail west.
- The trail along Valley View Rd. narrows west of Round Lake and is crossed by a number of residential streets. Some experienced riders may prefer to ride along the low-traffic road instead of the designated trail.
- Turn left at Dell Rd. to follow the adjoining bike path south to the intersection with the Minnesota River Bluffs Regional Trail.
- A right turn onto the gravel-paved Minnesota River Bluffs Regional Trail brings you to the rest stop at Riley Lake Park. If you don't want a rest stop, or would prefer to stay off of the gravel, just continue south along Dell Rd. to Pioneer Tr.

Rest Stop ✋**:** Riley Lake Park (mile 8.0), 9180 Riley Lake Rd., Eden Prairie, 55347. Amenities include portable latrines, a picnic shelter, drinking fountains, and a swimming beach.

- From the picnic shelter, ride south along the lake on the bike path until it merges with Riley Lake Rd. Follow Riley Lake Rd. to the park entrance on Pioneer Tr. Turn left onto the bike path along Pioneer Tr. and follow it for about 2.5 miles to Staring Lake Park, just across the street from Flying Cloud Airport. Staring Lake Park is close to the end of the ride but makes a great stop if you need a rest, or just like to watch airplanes!
- Follow the bike path to Staring Lake, past the picnic shelter, and down the hill behind the playground. At the bottom of the hill, turn right to circle counterclockwise around Staring Lake.
- At the north end of the lake, turn right onto the park entrance road, then right again onto the bike trail along Staring Lake Pkwy. for about a block.
- At the trail crossing, turn left to cross Staring Lake Pkwy. and get to the trail along Purgatory Creek.
- After 0.5 mile, turn right to cross over Purgatory Creek, then follow the trail counterclockwise around the wetland to return to the start.

Points of Interest ➡ : The Dorenkemper House (rest stop). Located about 100 yards north of the picnic shelter in Riley Lake Park, the Dorenkemper House is an example of pioneer architecture. Likely built in the 1850s, this

log-framed house has its original straw and mud chinking and is covered with clapboard siding on the outside and plaster on the inside.

Round Lake Park (mile 3.5) has nice facilities and a convenience store across the street if you want a short break early in the ride.

Flying Cloud Airport (mile 11) was once the second-busiest airport in the central United States, after Chicago-O'Hare. Originally built in 1941 to train Navy pilots, the airport now mostly serves small private planes. The main runways are visible from Staring Lake Park.

Staring Lake Park (mile 11) has picnic tables and restrooms available if you need to rest up before the final 3 miles. Don't worry, it's all downhill or flat from here.

Extended Activities:

- The Eden Prairie Outdoor Center (mile 12.3) is located on the north shore of Staring Lake, 13765 Staring Lake Pkwy., Eden Prairie, 55347. The Outdoor Center offers a variety of outdoor recreation and environmental education classes, workshops and activities. Acclaimed author and wildlife photographer Stan Tekiela is the naturalist at this center.

Jon's Notes: Eden Prairie is a thriving community and was rated as the "Best Place to Live" in America by *Money* magazine in 2010. Its excellent network of parks and trails is part of what makes it stand out. Eden Prairie boasts 170 miles of multiuse trails, many of which are great for family bike rides.

When I was growing up, my dad and I would sometimes take long bike rides out through the western suburbs. Flying Cloud Airport, located high on the bluffs overlooking the Minnesota River, marked our turnaround point. Sometimes we would linger for a while along Pioneer Trail to watch the planes take off and land before we headed home. You may want to do the same.

Purgatory in Eden Trail Environment

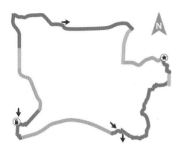

The "feel" of this route

YELLOW—urban areas or along busy streets
BLUE—suburban areas or neighborhoods
GREEN—parks, parkways and rural or natural settings

GPS Coordinates

⊛ Start/End (Purgatory Creek Park): 44° 51' 31.42" N 93° 26' 24.06" W

⊛ Rest Stop (Lake Riley Park): 44° 50' 13.35" N 93° 30' 40.15" W

→ Point of Interest (Round Lake Park): 44° 52' 9.32" N 93° 29' 17.45" W

→ Point of Interest (Dorenkemper House): 44° 50' 18.63" N 93° 30' 41.47" W

→ Point of Interest (Staring Lake Park): 44° 50' 4.91" N 93° 27' 47.34" W

→ Point of Interest (Flying Cloud Airport): 44° 49' 45.98" N 93° 26' 59.65" W

About the Author

Jonathan Poppele is a naturalist, author and educator with wide-ranging interests. He holds a master's degree in Conservation Biology and has taught ecology, environmental studies, biology and technical writing at the University of Minnesota. An avid outdoorsman and silent sport enthusiast, Jon began cycling the roads and bike trails around the Twin Cities as a young child and has logged tens of thousands of miles of pedaling over the past 35 years. As an amateur bike racer in the early 1990s, Jon won a state games championship, earned a national ranking in the match sprint, and competed in the U.S. Olympic Trials. Long retired from racing, he now rides for fun and for transportation, commuting about 2,500 miles each year on his bike. A personal development coach and a Black Belt in the peaceful martial art of Ki-Aikido, Jon is also the founder and Director of the Center for Mind-Body Oneness in Saint Paul, MN. He can be contacted through his website at www.jonathanpoppele.com.